Power in Practice

Power in Practice
The Pragmatic Anthropology of Afro-Brazilian Capoeira

Sergio González Varela

berghahn
NEW YORK · OXFORD
www.berghahnbooks.com

Published in 2017 by

Berghahn Books

www.berghahnbooks.com

Library of Congress Cataloging-in-Publication Data

Names: Gonzalez Varela, Sergio Armando, author.
Title: Power in practice : the pragmatic anthropology of Afro-Brazilian
    capoeira / Sergio Gonzalez Varela.
Description: New York : Berghahn Books, 2017. | Includes bibliographical
    references and index.
Identifiers: LCCN 2017017958 (print) | LCCN 2017029775 (ebook) | ISBN
    9781785336362 (e-book) | ISBN 9781785336355 (hardback : alk. paper)
Subjects: LCSH: Capoeira (Dance)—Anthropological aspects. | Blacks—
    Brazil—Social life and customs.
Classification: LCC GV1796.C145 (ebook) | LCC GV1796.C145 G66 2017
    (print) | DDC 792.80981—dc23
LC record available at https://lccn.loc.gov/2017017958

British Library Cataloguing-in-Publication Data

A catalogue record for this book is available from the British Library

ISBN 978-1-78533-635-5 (hardback)
ISBN 978-1-78533-636-2 (ebook)

DEDICATION

To Kasia

✵ Contents

❧ Illustrations

Tables

ꙮ Acknowledgments

This book is based on my involvement in the world of capoeira since 1999. I thank the Consejo Nacional de Ciencia y Tecnología (National Council on Science and Technology) in Mexico for financial support while I studied at University College London for the period 2004–8; this support allowed me to do extensive research in Salvador, Bahia, Brazil, in the years 2005 and 2006. For extra funding to complete my research in Brazil I thank the Graduate School Research Projects Funds at University College London. This book could not have been completed without the support of the Facultad de Ciencias Sociales y Humanidades (Faculty of Social Sciences and Humanities) at the Universidad Autónoma de San Luis Potosí, Mexico, which has been my academic home since 2010.

University College London has been at the forefront of anthropological research for many years and this book has benefited from that academic environment. I thank my graduate supervisors Allen Abramson and Martin Holbraad who encouraged me to write about capoeira and to pursue an academic career focused on the themes of ritual, performance, and ontology; they were and continue to be a source of inspiration in my life. My sincere respect goes to Victoria Goddard and Bruce Kapferer; both presented me with a new perspective about my work, and their criticism and comments helped me to improve substantially the manuscript of the book. I owe to many colleagues their critical feedback to some of the draft chapters of the book presented in conferences in Europe, The United States, Mexico and Chile, particularly Emiliano Zolla Márquez, Diana Espirito Santo, Marjorie Murray, José Luis Pérez Flores, Enrique Delgado, Jerome Lewis, David Napier, Rodney Reynolds, Piero DiGiminiani, Carlo Bonfiglioli, Isabel Martínez, Alejandro Fujigaki Lares, Anahí Luna, Iván Pérez Téllez, Leopoldo Trejo, Johannes Neurath, Antonio Reyes, Olivia Kindl, Arturo Gutiérrez del Ángel, Ángel Lacona, Rodrigo Díaz Cruz, Gabriela Vargas-Cetina, Pedro Ovando, Anne Johnson, Adriana Guzmán, Annelou Ypeij, Menara Guizardi, Inger Sjorslev, Nico Tassi, Cristobal Bonelli, Helene Risor, and Elizabeth Povinelli. I thank Eduardo Viveiros de Castro who in 2005 made an academic affiliation possible for me at the Museu Nacional de Rio de Janeiro; his brief but important advice was of much help during my stay in Brazil.

Many people and friends offered their support during my research in Brazil. Along the years, I have met incredible people who have helped me in one way or another to better understand the world of capoeira. In Bahia, I thank Mestre Boca do Rio and his Grupo Zimba, Mestres Valmir Damasceno and Cobra Mansa and their group Fundação Internacional de Capoeira Angola (FICA; International Capoeira Angola Foundation), Mestre Renê and his academy Associação de Capoeira Angola Navio Negreiro (ACANNE; Slave Ship Capoeira Angola Association), and Mestre Poloca and his academy Grupo Nzinga for opening the doors of their schools, and for giving me their support, confidence, and trust. Jair Moura, Eugênio Soares, Adriana Albert Dias, Matthias Assunção, Christine Zonzon, and the late Frederico de Abreu taught me the value of capoeira as an Afro-Brazilian martial art form, and their investigations have had a strong influence in the way I see the history and anthropology of capoeira Angola today; I have just words of gratitude to them. My special thanks go to all the *mestres* of capoeira Angola I had the opportunity to interview and talk to in Bahia.

I thank my friends Márcio de Abreu, Chris Johnson, Roque Bomfim-Batista de Jesús, Daniel Ribeiro Mattar, Cristina Olivera, Mestre Carlão, Contramestre Marcelo Peçanha, Contramestre Rogerio Serrote, Toca Feliciano Peçanha, George Howell, Juliet Line, Curtis Fell, Sophie Sakmann, Susana, Fabricio (FICA), Jack Hurrell, Patrick Higgins, Paula Andreewitch, Elina Hartikainen, Jagad, Adolfo Flores and his group Longe do Mar, Alejandro Ruiz, Uriel Mancilla Reyna, Ivette García García, and the *capoeiristas* from Ilha de Itaparica. A special place is reserved to Claudio Madureira, Christine Eida Madureira, and their daughter Roama, whose hospitality made me feel at home at the Largo Dois de Julho. I owe to Iñaki Garrido my first classes of capoeira in Mexico; he was and continues to be one of the most authentic capoeira teachers I have ever had.

Thanks to two anonymous reviewers for Berghahn Books who provided me with important and productive comments that gave invaluable insight to the book, and to Marion Berghahn, the editor in chief, for her trust in my project, and to her editorial staff for their patient and dedicated work during the production of the book.

The final draft of this book was completed while I worked as visiting professor at West Chester University, Pennsylvania. I owe mainly to Paul Stoller his support and interest in my book; I thank him, and all the academic and administrative staff at the Department of Anthropology and Sociology at West Chester University, for their incredible effort in making me feel at home in Pennsylvania; my deep gratitude for their generous assistance.

I would like to thank my family for their love and support during all these years: to my parents—my mother Cristina and my father José Manuel—my brother José Edgar, his wife Marcela Pombo, and little Sebastián, and to the families of González Padilla and Soto Varela my sincere appreciation and deep gratitude. Finally, I thank my wife Kasia who has been my partner in crime for almost ten years and has followed the development of this book since its inception; to her all my love. A last word to our little daughter Natasza who has brought us happiness and much love; she provides the necessary motivation to continue writing and teaching anthropology.

ꙮ Preface

I was in Mexico City the first time I heard about capoeira. It was 1999, and I was an undergraduate student at the Escuela Nacional de Antropología e Historia (National School of Anthropology). I had been spending long hours at my desk writing. To battle this sedentary lifestyle, I searched for a sportive activity that would engage my body and vent the stress produced by academic life. More and more, I felt as if my body were completely divorced from my mind.

While visiting a cultural center in the Coyoacán neighborhood, my eye was caught by a small, bright-yellow leaflet pinned to one of the walls. The leaflet advertised capoeira classes twice a week. There was a vague explanation about the meaning of capoeira being an art created by runaway slaves in Brazil, accompanied by an image of two human silhouettes doing handstands. Although I have forgotten most of the information provided in the leaflet, I remember one fact clearly, even to this day: at the bottom of the leaflet was written the assertion that the person in charge of the classes had learned capoeira from an "authentic" Brazilian master.

I decided to pay a visit to the place advertised on the leaflet—a sudden impulse that seemed to be the perfect solution to my woes. The moment I arrived at the class, I was instantly captivated by capoeira; the acrobatic bodily movements were mesmerizing, the music was seductive, and the way the students interacted was one of camaraderie and respect. Even then, though, I could not have imagined what this decision would bring to my life, even just a few years later.

I started training capoeira in Mexico City on a regular basis. I began with a Mexican instructor and later found a Brazilian *mestre* (a Brazilian teacher): Pedrinho de Caxias. He had been a well-known figure in the capoeira scene of Rio de Janeiro, his home city, and he was a teacher of the Angola[1] style. To train with a true *mestre* in Mexico in 2001 was something rare, because the country had never provided an economic hub attractive enough to entice the famous leaders of capoeira to move.

Although many *mestres* had visited Mexico, Pedrinho was one of the first to live there permanently.

Meeting Pedrinho was another experience that marked my life. He was a very charming man with a strong personality that fluctuated from wise and fatherly to fearsome. He brought together a strong and committed group of students, not only in Mexico but also in Argentina, where he had lived before. I did not know anything about capoeira Angola before meeting Pedrinho, but after three years of practicing capoeira with him, I began to glimpse the foundations of the style. I learned as much as I could from Pedrinho before I left for Europe in 2002.

I continued training after that, first in Sweden and later in England. In both countries, I was fortunate to meet more *mestres* of capoeira Angola. I took classes and workshops with them and attended a variety of events in other European cities, as well. In 2005, as part of my graduate studies, I traveled for the first time to the city of Salvador, Bahia, in the northeast of Brazil, to carry out research.

In the city of Salvador, in the state of Bahia, my perception of capoeira leaders changed. Their influence and power was more evident and overbearing than I had previously experienced in Mexico and Europe. In Bahia *mestres* of the Angola style had a prestigious position within the Afro-Brazilian community. An attitude of reverence to these persons pervaded every interaction I had with members of the capoeira Angola groups. Local people regarded them as persons of knowledge. This initial realization had profound implications concerning the aims of my research.

My fascination with the *mestres* led me to ask myself why they had become so powerful, admired, and respected. My research revealed only after a few months that capoeira Angola could not be understood without referring to the Bahia *mestres*. Everything in capoeira seemed to revolve around them: they were the focal point for the community of participants, they were responsible for many of the historical changes that capoeira had undergone throughout the twentieth century, and their oral tradition was a constant reminder of the role that old *mestres* had played, both in the configuration of modern capoeira practice and in the preservation of what they called their Afro-Brazilian heritage.

I got to know many *mestres* and I became a constant presence in the capoeira Angola scene of Bahia during the years 2005 and 2006. Because I had come to Bahia both as a researcher and a practitioner of capoeira, I learned the hard way many of the insights that appear in this book. Participation became a daily battle to master a physical and mental activity that was strenuous and exhausting, due mainly to the tropical weather conditions. My understanding of capoeira became very different from my understanding in Mexico and Europe. The difference resided in my close contact with the *mestres* and the many hours of interviews, classes, and informal conversations I had with them. By the end of my fifteen-month research period, there were only three *mestres* whom I got to know closely enough to consider my friends.

Not everybody was receptive to my research or willing to share their knowledge with me. There is a tradition of secrecy in capoeira Angola, and knowledge is not shared openly; in some cases, it is not desirable to reveal things. In part because learning capoeira is unsystematic and based on practice, people are very careful to confide only in those whom they trust.

Time plays an important role in developing skills and knowledge and it does not stop when one becomes a *mestre*. "Capoeira Angola is an endless source of knowledge," said Mestre Boca do Rio, who was one of my friends. It is not possible to give a full account of all the elements that form even part of the world of this art form. What I describe in these pages is an account based on my interactions with *mestres* of capoeira Angola and advanced students. It attempts to portray the perspective that leaders have about their art. At the same time, it builds up an anthropological argument on power and practice from their point of view. It is also a book about social relations and the contextual situations that emerge from the agency of a powerful subject (the *mestre*), and discusses the process of learning to become powerful. It describes the effects of power in the configuration of hierarchies and structures within capoeira Angola groups and analyzes the repercussions of this practice on the bodies of its participants.

My aim is to provide an anthropological account of power from a *mestre's* perspective, based both on their experience and on my partial knowledge of capoeira. In this writing, I have tried to remain closer to the world that was revealed to me, and I hope that I have been faithful to it. Many capoeira Angola players may or may not agree with my perspective on their art; this is one of the tricks that capoeira plays. Because capoeira is conceived by practitioners to be holistic—because it encompasses everything—what one perceives or is being told by *mestres* is simply just a glimpse, an incomplete account of a mysterious and astonishing social practice that seems to be always one step ahead of our total comprehension. With this in mind, I apologize if I have misinterpreted or misunderstood the perspective of the *mestres* in the pages that follow. Any such errors must lie at my own feet.

Notes

1. There are three styles of capoeira: capoeira Angola, capoeira Contemporânea (Contemporary), and capoeira Regional. Chapter 2 will describe the distinction among these styles as part of the historical background of capoeira's development. The concepts outlined in this book deal specifically with capoeira Angola.

✨ Introduction

I was tempted to quit capoeira once and for all following a grueling class with Mestre Boca do Rio, the leader of Grupo Zimba in Salvador, Brazil. I was frustrated to feel that I was not improving after seven years of dedicating my life to the practice of capoeira Angola. Every time I played with Boca, I just couldn't get anything past him. He was too experienced and was always one step ahead of me. To make matters worse, in the *rodas* (weekly gatherings) of the group, I was always afraid of playing with him, even though I knew him very well and we were friends. My fear in the *roda* also extended to other *mestres* and advanced practitioners—not to all, of course, but to a great majority of them. Why was I afraid? What situations did capoeira create around these persons that made me feel hopeless and filled with fear?

I shared my feeling with Boca days later, after he convinced me not to quit capoeira. He mentioned that it was normal to feel afraid when facing a *mestre* or somebody with more experience. Fear was part of a student's apprenticeship. This strange feeling of fear came out of respect and deference to a person who has more knowledge than you, he said. He also said that fear was the evidence of power. Even he felt a great apprehension any time somebody mentioned the name of his *mestre*, Moraes, even though he had cut all ties with the *mestre* in 1996 and they had not spoken since.

To hear that Boca do Rio, a skilled capoeira *mestre* who instills such respect in others, was also subject to the same fear that I experienced made me wonder about how far and deep go the power relations that exist among leaders, particularly among those who dedicate their lives to teach and practice capoeira as a way of life. What connections, divisions, alliances, and disputes does capoeira Angola create?

The story of Boca do Rio is a good example of the hard path of apprenticeship for a person who decides to become a *mestre*. He started capoeira at a young age and, in the mid 1980s, decided to enroll at the Grupo de Capoeira Angola Pelourinho (GCAP; Capoeira Angola Group from Pelourinho). He was a member of GCAP until 1996, when he abandoned the group.

In the 1980s the practice of capoeira Angola was very different. According to Boca, there were just a few practicing groups and players worked closely with their *mestres*. The *mestres* did not spend half of the year traveling all over the world, as they do today. In some cases, members considered their groups to be their extended family, with the *mestres* taking the roles of mentors and guides. Boca, together with other students who are now famous *mestres,* learned the GCAP way, which includes strict discipline, rigor, and self-awareness of the importance of being part of an Afro-Brazilian tradition. All of these persons started from scratch, as nobodies in a world that historically and systematically discriminated against them. Part of the success of these individuals can be traced back to their training with the GCAP under the command of Mestre Moraes. There were other *mestres* at the time, including João Grande, João Pequeno, and Cobra Mansa, but Boca and the other GCAP members considered Moraes to be the most influential *mestre* in their lives.

Boca do Rio was one of the last members of the 1980s generation to leave the group. One by one, all these excellent players either deserted the GCAP because of the overbearing personality of Moraes or because Moraes expelled them. They formed new groups and cut all ties with their *mestre*. Boca never wanted to leave the GCAP, but said that he was forced to. Moraes was a charismatic figure and an imposing one. Control was exhibited via a nonnegotiable set of rules with which all members of his academy had to abide. Respect to the *mestre* became a synonym for blind deference.

The separation was not amicable. Moraes accused many of his ex-students of betrayal, of leaving the true path of capoeira Angola to pursue selfish interests. Today, he does not consider them to be true bearers of the capoeira Angola tradition, and he did not grant them the titles of *mestres*. It was not until the mid 2000s that Boca and his peers were finally rewarded with the titles of *mestre* by their other mentor of capoeira Angola at GCAP, Mestre Cobra Mansa, who had also left the group in 1994.

This broken chain of power is not uncommon in the capoeira Angola academies I studied. I have collected many similar stories that show the complexities of the *mestre*–student relationship in Salvador, Rio de Janeiro, and elsewhere. Although there is no single cause that could explain the way *mestres* behave with their students, in all cases the power of the *mestres* is not disputed by the members of the group. People who do not belong to the group may question the authority and the moral grounds of certain *mestres,* but within these academies nobody doubts the *mestre.* The *mestre's* power is evident, unquestionable, and always demonstrated in practice and performance, which are means of instilling not only respect and admiration, but also fear. Power is, in essence, pragmatic.

Power in Practice

Some of the most important issues discussed in this book relate to the themes of power, adherence to a tradition, deference, practice, and the dialectics between the individual and the collective. In essence, the book is about the concept of power and how it is conceived, learned, and performed by capoeira Angola *mestres.* My main argument states that, in order to understand the world of capoeira Angola, one must necessarily focus on the cosmological and practical connotations of power and how power shapes social relations. I argue that focusing the argument of the book on power provides a better comprehension about the process of transmitting knowledge and consolidating an Afro-Brazilian tradition in a globalized world.

I describe power relations, knowledge, and tradition from the point of view of the *mestres.* Although I often talk generally about *mestres* as if they were all the same, the word has to be considered heuristically because it denotes a diversity of contrasting personal views and attitudes about capoeira Angola.

To base a book on the role played by powerful leaders implies a male-centered perspective, since the vast majority of capoeira Angola leaders are men. However, women do take part in the practice and are as important in today's capoeira groups as any other practitioner.[1] There is at least one group led mainly by women—Grupo Nzinga.[2] The leaders of Grupo Nzinga have strived to attain recognition of women as figures of power in capoeira.[3] In other cases in Salvador and elsewhere, women play a huge role in the development and preservation of the Angola tradition. The influence of foreign students has been of extreme importance in the slow process of recognizing gender equality in capoeira, although this process has never run smoothly and is not easily accepted by many male leaders (see Griffith 2016).

My ethnography follows a tradition in capoeira studies influenced mainly by the classic works of Lowell Lewis (1992) and Greg Downey

(2005), two of the most prominent anthropologists in the capoeira research field. I argue that Lewis's and Downey's approaches, although of great value, omit relevant aspects that need to be addressed. In the case of Greg Downey, he does not explicitly describe the conflicting social relations and internal hierarchical politics of the practice, which results in a narrative favoring a more experiential and individual account of the practice that does not give full justice to the specificities of the local political milieu of capoeira academies. There is nothing wrong with an experiential approach in anthropology, but the experience must be connected to the realm of local social relations in order to become more meaningful.

Lewis, on the other hand, contends that capoeira should be viewed as a text to be interpreted based on a semiotic framework. Although I sympathize with the different levels of signification analyzed by Lewis, I suggest that an analytical approach to capoeira runs the risk of diminishing the importance of difference and the practical and cosmological contrast of styles. I believe that attending to the specificities of every style will bring our understanding closer to the local anthropological perspective of capoeira.

In the growing bibliography available on capoeira, one commonly finds that style differentiation does not play an essential analytical role (Araújo Caires 2006; Barbosa 2005a, 2005b; Hedegard 2012; MacLennan 2011; Rector 2008; Reis 2000). This does not mean that academics are unaware of these differences; other studies show how capoeira has been divided into styles and consider Regional, Contemporary, and Angola modalities in a context of global expression (Delamont and Stephens 2007, 2008; Falcão 2005; Farias and Vilodre 2007; Fonseca 2008; Griffith 2016; Guizardi 2011; Magalhães 2011).

In some cases, differentiation may not play a part in the development of an author's theoretical argument, and thus that author is justified in not considering the different modalities. In many ways, some of the assumptions I make could be easily applied to any capoeira style. In other ways, it is crucial to consider the distinct aspects of capoeira Angola.

I conceive capoeira Angola as building a world in itself because of the particular positioning of capoeira Angola *mestres* compared to *mestres* in other styles. In Salvador I found that *mestres* make a clearcut differentiation between the Angola style they practice and the styles practiced by capoeira Regional *mestres*. For Angola *mestres* this distinction is of paramount importance. Perceiving capoeira Angola as distinct from the other two styles is the starting point to analyzing the process of knowledge creation and to creating a description of the local tradition.

To focus on difference implies a statement in favor of radical alterity. By showing the particularities of capoeira Angola as a unifying practice, I intend to provide a total vision of this style. At the same time, I outline the issue of political discrepancy within capoeira Angola groups as a central aspect of the practice.

A World in Itself

Considering capoeira Angola as a world in itself means to see it in a holistic way. I take the idea from the perspective of the *mestres* with whom I worked. For them, capoeira Angola is an essential part of their lives: whatever they think, dream, and do is always connected to the practice of the Afro-Brazilian art. It looks as if *mestres* were suited with a particular and exclusive worldview that could not be shared with people who do not practice capoeira.

I consider capoeira Angola to be a ritual practice that can be explained in its own terms and in its own right. I take this stance from the work of Don Handelman and Galina Lindquist (2005), who argued that the scope of ritual can be understood in its own terms by focusing on the potential that certain ritual practices have to create particular worlds. Whether or not these worlds are real, the idea allows for the potential of any ritual to create its own reality. This potential is what Bruce Kapferer called "virtuality" (Kapferer 2007) when he described the capacity to make things creatively possible in ritual.

Explaining a ritual like capoeira Angola in its own terms means to conceive it beyond functional modes of explanation. Functional modes normally explain rituals by making them exclusively the products of more-general social causes. Under this view, ritual is seen as a cathartic phenomenon—a way of coping with stress, frustration, violence, anger, and so on.

My perspective runs against this functional and simplistic solution. I see capoeira as a microcosmos that contains social relations that, in many cases, exist in tension with the sociohistorical formation of Bahian society. It is common to find that *mestres* make extraordinary efforts to build a virtual barrier around capoeira in order to keep it separated from non-Afro-Brazilian practices. These efforts are perhaps a way of preserving a distinctive tradition. In a world where competition, tourism, and global influences play an important role in the success or failure of an academy, keeping a tradition close to its Afro-Brazilian roots is essential.

In recent years, however, the global exposure of the Angola style has reconfigured the way *mestres* interact with the world beyond the premises of their academies. They are at a crossroad that requires negotiating with followers of other styles and accommodating people who are interested in knowing the "secrets" of capoeira Angola. They also have to confront the competition and mistrust that exists among capoeira Angola practitioners.

Be that as it may, I find that the effort *mestres* make in order to create modes of identification among capoeira Angola practitioners is particularly important. In Salvador, *mestres* have been increasingly preoccupied with being considered the true caretakers of tradition, particularly among foreign students who wish to see the "real" capoeira Angola in one of its places of origin. By closing in on itself, capoeira Angola has been able to build up a context that is separate from other capoeira styles and Afro-Brazilian practices.

The Scope of Creativity: Dialectics between the Individual and the Collective

There is a dialectic oscillation between the individual power embodied by the *mestres* and the collective conventions of capoeira Angola formed by a community of participants. In this book I want to show the mutual interdependency between the individual and the collective in capoeira Angola without trying to solve anthropology's fundamental problem with the opposition between social constraints and individual action.[4] For example, the social context of capoeira is affected by the individual agency executed by a powerful person. This social context is formed by a collective tradition that dictates the structuring of groups should conform to hierarchies that recognize the holders of knowledge. This organization is vital to the power relations that *mestres* have with other individuals.

Interdependency between individual invention and collective conventions means that one part of the relation cannot exist without the other. This book emphasizes the part of the *mestres* and their individual, creative forms of powerful actions without neglecting the importance of the social collective conventions in which they are performed.[5] This dialectical move between the individual and the collective provides an excellent starting point for exploring the *mestres'* perceptions about their practice.

In general, *mestres* assume that their personal power is responsible for the collective forms of the game's inner social structure. Thus, for *mestres* of capoeira and their supporters, the inner power that shapes their own playful microcosm has its origin not in the all-encompassing structures and solidarity of Bahian society at large, but in a secretive and socially elusive magical source accessible only by themselves. I discuss this spiritual domain in detail during the description of the cosmological connotations of power in chapter 4. For the time being, it is enough to say that the *mestres'* self-perception defines the outcome of ritual actions as a thing that emerges from their creative engagement with the world.

In this sense, the creative power of the *mestres* evokes Hans Joas's pragmatic theory of creative action (Joas 1996), which holds that action is not something teleological or rationally motivated by normative schemes. For Joas,[6] action must be creative and phenomenologically uncertain concerning where it will lead. Although *mestres* may have an idea of the source of their power relations, they cannot control completely the outcomes and results of such actions and they cannot control the intentions of those who take actions against them. In chapter 3 we will see how this uncertain control serves as a platform to the concept of bodily closure as a form of protecting power.

The creative assumption of individual power and its dialectic negotiation with collective conventions is intrinsically related to the dialectic anthropology of Roy Wagner, who considers that the cornerstone of anthropology resides in the relationship between conventional and individual (nonconventional) models of symbolization (Wagner 1981).[7] Following Wagner, it is possible to identify the pole of individual invention with the body and power of a *mestre,* and perceive this identification as a unified, singular entity. The privileged way to show this power is by means of performance. It is in practice that a *mestre* displays his knowledge, reveals his powerful attributes, and defines his role as a man who belongs to a tradition.

This is why I consider the *mestres* of capoeira to be inventors of culture in Wagner's terms. They serve as mediators between conventional and nonconventional models of symbolization. They are individuals who see that their inner magical power is responsible for the creation of a community of practitioners and its existing rules. Therefore, at the interior of capoeira there is a power defined by its apparent social excess; this power is projected into the hierarchies that determine the relationships within Angola academies. By considering this excess to emerge from individual power, we can understand the vignette narrated at the beginning of the introduction, wherein Mestre Boca do Rio is describing as having felt the overbearing presence of his *mestre* to be oppressing and debilitating. Another form of powerful agency is expressed by the feeling of fear and frustration that individuals face when they have to deal with powerful adversaries in the *roda*.

The Nature of Power and Its Agency

Mestres see the social as an extension of themselves in the sense that they use their power to justify their transcendence of the hierarchy that they impose on others. One could call this power spiritual, supernatural, or charismatic (Weber 1922/1978: 241). It is a form of power that grows with time and experience. A *mestre* earns or accumulates his power through practicing capoeira and by getting involved in a certain religious context. Only on a few occasions did I hear remarks about *mestres* whose power was considered to be a part of their nature. On the contrary, a *mestre* becomes powerful through a long, ascetic process of apprenticeship. The apprenticeship includes suffering under the overbearing and excessive power of a prominent *mestre*.

A *mestre*, therefore, has the capacity to make others follow and respect him. His primary tools are his body and his knowledge, which are the containers of his power. Subsequently, it is in the practice of capoeira that a *mestre* makes evident his powerful attributes. As many *mestres* have told me, it is the quality of one's skills or music capabilities that determine the respect and admiration of others. The focus on the body as a source and receptacle of the magical and creative forces involved in performance transforms an initial metaphysical conception of power into a real, concrete fact that lacks transcendence: *mestres* are the embodiment of power.

Yet *mestres* must face leaders who are equally or more powerful. Therefore, rivalries emerge as a consequence of their social relations; these rivalries cause the formation of lineages. These lineages provide a mental and practical control following the practitioner's adscription to a particular tradition of knowledge. They act as a form of hierarchical differentiation, too. The supernatural origins of *mestres'* power is complemented by the collective forms of adscription represented by lines of descent.

By supernatural or spiritual power, I mean that certain energy goes beyond the materiality of *mestres'* bodies, but that is expressed through bodily action. This power is at once cosmological and pragmatic. To say that power is spiritual does not mean that it necessarily has its origin exclusively in Afro-Brazilian religions like Candomblé. In some cases, particularly with leaders who are practitioners of these religions, there is an evident connection between Candomblé and capoeira. Yet, there are Protestant and even evangelic *mestres* who are trying to remove from their practice any association with Afro-Brazilian religions, but who still ascribe spiritual powers to the practice of capoeira. In chapter 3 I will give a more detailed explanation of the links between capoeira and spirituality.

In practice, power has an agency that affects humans and nonhumans. Leaders consider this agency to be another way to make power evident. The agency of power blurs distinctions so that musical instruments may become persons who cry, send messages, and participate in a *mestre's* power, as I will show in chapter 6. Power also affects the feelings and emotions of adversaries; *mestres* instill fear, as I described earlier. They can make people sick or vulnerable. Agency is the way power operates as a marker for both those who have proper knowledge and those who do not. Therefore, agency is at the core of the dialectic move between the individual and the collective. It moves and transforms relations; it is ontologically designed and epistemologically assimilated. It emerges from the ritual scope of capoeira Angola, which is able to create a world in itself.

Organization of the Book

The book is organized into six chapters. Chapter 1 describes the history of capoeira Angola in Salvador, Bahia. The purpose of this historical description is to show how capoeira Angola became institutionalized in academies and structured as a distinctive practice. I pay particular attention to the role that *mestres* played in this historical process and how they assumed responsibility for how capoeira Angola has developed into the practice we see today. In the chapter I do not undertake a study about origins. I try to speculate as little as possible about the African sources of capoeira and focus more on the complementary dialogue between historians and capoeira experts. As much as I could, I tried to bring to light the struggles that *mestres* faced in order to consolidate their style in a world in which they were always considered a minority. The chapter thus also is a tale of the *mestres'* prowess and determination.

Chapter 2 focuses on the sociology of capoeira Angola groups in Salvador and their collective conventions. I delve into the scope of social relations, how a community of participants is created around the *mestres* in Salvador, and why the social aspects of this community are meaningful for anthropology. In the chapter I describe in detail the elements that make capoeira Angola a world in itself. My aim is to show the general structures of academies, as well as the relations that leaders have among themselves and with other practitioners. I also draw on the distinctiveness of capoeira Angola compared to the other capoeira styles (Regional and Contemporary) and the reasons behind this distinction. I define the capoeira Angola community (CAC) as a matrix composed by lineages that *mestres* use as a form of legitimation of belonging to a common tradition.

The objective of chapter 3[8] is to describe the relationship between embodiment, cosmology, and spirituality among capoeira Angola leaders. I draw on my ethnographic material and experience as practitioner for this purpose. The central focus of the chapter is on the process of learning capoeira and the arduous physical labor that this implies. I argue in favor of understanding capoeira by categorizing it under three main levels: embodiment, symbolic connotations of the body, and cosmological principles. My intention is not to describe how a novice or an initial student learns this ritual art form, but rather how an apprentice becomes a *mestre* and, subsequently, how a *mestre* sees the world from a position of power and knowledge. For this purpose I engage with the concept of the *corpo fechado* (closed body) as a local ethnographic concept that serves to make visible the connections between practice, cosmology, and embodiment. Finally, I describe the complex relation that exists between capoeira and Candomblé as belonging to a common plural cosmological matrix. In the case of capoeira Angola, Candomblé complements the practice's spiritual and religious foundations. I also note how the spirituality in capoeira differs from that of Candomblé in many aspects.

Chapter 4[9] analyzes the issue of power based on the ethnographic context of capoeira Angola academies. The chapter describes the concept of *mandinga* as an indigenous form of power. I argue that *mandinga* gives further proof of the importance of practice in a ritual art form, since this concept shapes social relations, bodily interactions, magic acts, and the definition of personhood. The argument of the chapter centers on the logic of deception as one of the exclusive ways of expressing *mandinga*. I describe how the previous discussion on cosmology and embodiment appears as the base on which *mandinga* becomes evident. I propose to see the effects of *mandinga* in the bodies of the *mestres* as an ethnographic strategy to discuss the ontology of deception as the principle of capoeira Angola's practice.

Chapter 5 discusses the violent and playful sides of capoeira Angola and the ethical scope of its practice. I engage with the concepts of symbolic violence, performance, and play, and discuss the conundrum that *mestres* face between deception and morality. On the one hand, playful violence entails simulation, cheating, and betrayal. On the other hand, it also implies a rejection of seriousness and a strategy of shrewdness and cunning that has been defined by Roberto DaMatta (1991) as a characteristically Brazilian trait through the concept of *malandragem* (roguery). In this chapter, I undertake a further analysis of deception and the kind of ethical framework it creates, as well as how *mestres* have dealt with deception in the past and in the present. I argue that playfulness brings an aesthetic expression of power through deception, which defines the pragmatic character of capoeira Angola.

The aim of chapter 6[10] is to show the importance of music in academies and in capoeira performances. My main concern in this last chapter is with materiality and the aesthetic effect that music produces in participants. I draw on recent anthropological discussions about the potential of material culture to redefine anthropology from relational and ontological perspectives. My objective is to show how particular musical instruments become persons and how the power of personification is crucial to understanding the relations that a *mestre* builds with his tradition. *Mestres* activate the power of personification and, through music, make evident their position in the hierarchy of knowledge. I see music as essential for the creation of an aesthetic perception of capoeira, as a key component of its magic and spiritual connotations, and as a thing that involves collective and individual forms of symbolization.

The overall aim of this book is not only to describe capoeira from the *mestres*' points of view, but also to show how individual power shapes the configuration of a community of participants. My central point is to highlight the importance of ritual practice in the development of an ethnographic strategy that takes seriously the key role of capoeira leaders. I consider that power is elicited through creative action and shown to others; performance is the means by which a *mestre* convinces, entices, and (ultimately) deceives the opponent.

Notes

1. In order to stress the relevance of women in capoeira Angola, I use the feminine or masculine third person pronoun when I talk about members of the groups.
2. This name is from the Angolan African queen Anna Nzinga, who is considered to be an icon against oppression.
3. Relevant to the discussion of gender relations in capoeira are the important works of Araújo Caires 2006; Barbosa 2005a; Griffith 2016; Guizardi 2011; Hedegard 2012; Joseph 2005; and Zonzon 2014. Their works not only show in detail the way relations exist between men and women in capoeira groups, but also highlight the importance of a female perspective on capoeira studies, which is something that, until recently, was marginal and rare.
4. It is not easy to give a definitive statement about the level, quality, and intensity of the mutual influences among the collective conventions of society and the individual invention of culture. On the one hand, a social determinacy over individual actions and behaviors, like the traditional sociological approach of Durkheim (1995), could undermine the agency that individual actors have over the structures in which they live. On the other hand, a voluntaristic approach, like the one proposed by Nigel Rapport (2003), might run the risk of overshadowing the cultural and social conformations that limit the individual's freedom of action; this would transform anthropology into a by-product of psychological and mental categories. Opposing the collective to the individual leads us to this kind of cul-de-sac.
5. I am not suggesting what Bourdieu (1989) argues, that the relation between the individual and the collective is based on a dialectical form of social structuring. According to Bourdieu, it is possible to conceptualize structure as the armature of individual action, and thus the constraining field of categories in a social field is a condition of interaction for individuals but does not determine the outcomes of these interactions (Bourdieu 1989: 18). By developing the concept of habitus, Bourdieu seems to have overcome the problem of the individual and the collective. Although he is trying to reconcile both domains, the concept of habitus offers only a virtual conception of individual freedom. He seems to give primacy to the collective structuring force of the habitus as an a priori ordered predisposition.
6. I would like to thank an anonymous reviewer for suggesting that I refer to Joas's book, the existence of which I was unaware. I agree completely with his argument in favor of creative action as a feasible argument in which to situate the dialectic of the collective and the individual.

7. In my view, the intelligibility of capoeira resides exactly between the realms of conventional and nonconventional models of symbolization. I define a nonconventional or differentiating model of symbolization as the directly creative invocation of a resemblance between the symbol and its reference, while in the social creation of conventional contexts, arbitrariness establishes an ontological distance between the symbol and the symbolized. Although aspects of the conventional mode are important to the development of capoeira, many of the existing social relations seem to depend on nonconventional symbolizations created by *mestres*. This nonconventional form of symbolization has its origin in the evidence of power inscribed in the bodies of the leaders.

8. Part of the material in chapter 3 has been published before in Spanish in González Varela 2012a. Part of the subsection "The Logic of Practice: Learning about the Closed Body" is taken from González Varela 2013.

9. Parts of the material in chapter 4 has been published previously, although it has been edited for the purposes of this book (González Varela 2013).

10. Some of the topics discussed on materiality in chapter 6 were published previously in González Varela 2012.

CHAPTER 1

֍ The Fight for Recognition
A Brief History of Capoeira Angola in Salvador, Bahia, Brazil

The history of capoeira Angola in Bahia is relatively short: no more than ninety years have passed since the form was first introduced. This chapter tells that history in a way that puts the *mestres* of capoeira at the center of the narrative. My intention is to build my narrative around the stories and deeds of these powerful individuals, because I consider them to be essential shapers of the modern configuration of the Afro-Brazilian tradition of capoeira. Because *mestres* are the main protagonists in this reconstruction of the past, I aim to give them a voice in the creation of this history. The last two sections of this chapter, particularly, focus on the *mestres'* perspectives.

It is important to mention that *mestres'* narratives about the past contrast sharply with the current historical narrative. I do not intend to resolve the existing tensions between local narratives and the formal historical work produced by academics, however, because the problem is not one that can be cleared up easily. Instead, I intend to offer a poetics of epic acts that includes both the narratives of *mestres* and the information found in the increasing historiography of capoeira. The exploration does not require veracity or confirmation that the stories told really happened. This honors what Stephan Palmié and Charles Stewart (2016) have named "new forms of historicity," in which non-Western people offer valuable and innovative forms of narrating the past by means of performance, dance, bodies in movement, and images. These narratives may or may not be in agreement with the narratives created by professional approaches to academic history. However, their value resides in producing other forms of knowledge and understandings of the past that have not yet been considered. By combining historical data with information provided by *mestres,* I bring to light a narrative about capoeira Angola's history in a form that gives justice to both sources.

A Violent Past: Capoeira in Bahia before 1930

According to historian Matthias Röhrig Assunção (Assunção 2005: 96–128), there are no records of capoeira Angola, and very little about capoeira in general, before 1936. The lack of information about capoeira during this period impedes discussion about the development of capoeira in Bahia during the first half of the nineteenth century. Currently, the only documents at hand referencing capoeira are one 1835 painting depicting a capoeira fight, created by artist Johann Moritz Rugendas, and a narrative found in James Wetherell's personal diary in 1856. The narrative, as it appears in the translation published by Assunção (2005), is, "Negroes fighting with their open hands is a frequent scene in the lower city. They seldom come to blows, or at least sufficient to cause any serious damage. A kick on the shins is about the most painful knock they give each other. They are full of action, capering and throwing their arms and legs about like monkeys during their quarrels. It is a ludicrous sight" (Wetherell 1856, quoted and translated by Assunção 2005: 101).

The first explicit newspaper mention of capoeira, according to Assunção (2005), dates back to 1866. The newspaper associates the practice with gangs formed by *moleques* (black youngsters), whom authorities accused of creating disorder (ibid.: 102). A subsequent series of notes in newspapers show the gradually increasing presence of capoeira in Bahian society. These mentions emphasize the practice's urban character, the active role played by black people, and its use by gangs fighting for control and power in different neighborhoods of Salvador. During this early period, there is no evidence suggesting capoeira was a game or art form.

After the abolition of slavery in Brazil on 13 May 1888 and the proclamation of the First Republic (known also as the Old Republic) in Brazil in November 1889, there began gradual changes toward the creation of a national identity. Although these defining moments influenced the destiny of Brazil, they did not have the same impact in Salvador. According to historian Antonio Risério, slavery was no longer a profitable activity in the city in the 1870s, and the number of slaves sharply decreased year by year until there were only three thousand slaves within a total population of 120,000 by 1888; once abolition was proclaimed, those remaining slaves went to the city of Salvador either to find work in the docks or to try their luck in odd jobs (Risério 2004: 403). Bahia was one of the last states to acknowledge the legitimation of the Republic, and politicians appeared to consider the new regime with suspicion, due to the ongoing conflicts of power occurring in the south of the country (Risério 2004: 406).

These two facts had direct repercussions in the configuration of modern Brazilian society, and had an influence on capoeira, too. Abolition created an influx of free individuals who had to be inserted into the economy of the city, a fact that completely changed the cultural urban configuration of Salvador; as unemployment surged, those free slaves conformed a new class of dispossessed individuals with little opportunities to get a formal job, destined to roam the streets looking for informal jobs or any strategy of survival. In addition, the First Republic planted the seeds of a nationalist ideology that would guide the destiny of Brazil in the coming decades. The incipient ideas of modernity and progress compelled the inclusion of black individuals into society, but this was a very difficult project for the Republic, which faced racist and prejudiced ideologies from the elites and the government, which seemed fascinated with the imposition of positivism as a social and political doctrine.

As a predominantly Afro-Brazilian community, Bahia suffered from discriminatory policies. At the turn of the twentieth century, capoeira was linked mainly to criminals, vagrants, and rogues. Josivaldo Pires de Oliveira and Luiz Augusto Pinheiro Leal mention that authorities viewed with contempt those who practiced capoeira; those authorities made an incredible effort to eradicate this urban expression of "idleness and unproductiveness," (2009: 49–50). The penal code of the First Republic in 1890 prohibited formally the practice of capoeira in public places, although there are no documents in police records to prove that persons were detained for performing capoeira (see Dias 2006).

Oliveira (2005) describes the strong relationship between capoeira practitioners and their social environment during 1912–30. In some places of the city center, like the Praça da Sé, the Baixa dos Sapateiros, and Praça da Piedade, practitioners had an active presence in the streets. At night, the center became a hub for so-called marginal characters: drunkards, prostitutes, pimps, rogues, vagrants, vandals, and trouble-makers who wandered the streets looking for action, and, in some cases, looking for trouble with the authorities. Although most capoeira practitioners were Afro-Brazilians, there were always members of other social groups, including mulattoes, foreigners, whites, and people from southern Brazil.[1]

These characters were part of a subculture that lived a parallel, alternative, and opposite life to the principles established by the Republic. They had their own codes and strategies of survival in a hostile environment. They were streetwise negotiators who had very complex relations with local authorities. They could openly defy the police, while paying bribes to secure their protection.

According to Oliveira, the presence of these marginal characters became a social problem that threatened the stability and tranquility of the privileged Bahian elites. Authorities fought against the presence of vagrants, vagabonds, and criminals in the streets, and *vagabundagem* (vagrancy) was prohibited and strongly penalized. According to Oliveira (2005), "The person accused of vagrancy would have a deadline of fifteen days to prove that he exercised any form of legal work" (48).

The association between vagrancy and capoeira was strong. In fact, the two words were synonyms at the time; practitioners of capoeira indistinctly described the activity as *vadiação* (another word for vagrancy). Many capoeira practitioners did not have regular jobs, although they engaged in a diversity of sporadic jobs, and some of them had none. Historian Adriana Albert Dias lists about eleven types of work that capoeira players were likely to do, such as weight laborers, stevedores, anglers, sailors, and, surprisingly, police officers (Dias 2004: 41). This list shows that capoeira practitioners were not always challenging and confronting authorities, nor being challenged or confronted by authorities. In many cases practitioners could negotiate with or seek the help of local police officers.

According to Albert Dias, there are no detailed descriptions of the way people played capoeira before 1930. Newspapers did not give accounts of the musical or physical aspects of capoeira meetings (Dias 2004: 46). However, *mestres* compiled written registers during that period, and these mention the existence of capoeira gatherings—or, as Brazilians call them, *rodas*. Mestres like Mestre Noronha (Daniel Coutinho, 1909–1977) and Mestre Pastinha (Vicente Ferreira Pastinha, 1899–1981) were, perhaps, the first capoeira practitioners to leave written records of their experiences, ideas, and views on capoeira. These records form part of the authoritative documents describing the world of capoeira in the first decades of the twentieth century. For example, the manuscripts of Mestre Noronha served as a valuable source to build understanding of the social environment of capoeira in 1910–30 (Coutinho 1993). Thanks to him, people got to know capoeira practitioners such as Caboclinho, Nozinho, Tico, Pedro Mineiro, Olho de Pombo, Chico Tres Pedaços, and Pedro Porreta—individuals who otherwise would have faded from memory.

The scant newspaper information, combined with *mestres'* narratives, shows that capoeira before 1930 was at the core of an extraordinary mixture of violent accounts and problems with authorities and between gangs. Capoeira was an activity for tough guys; they were *valentes* (brave), *maliciosos* (tricky, malicious), *disordeiros* (troublemakers), *malandros* (rogues), and *criminais* (criminals). The available information in books and oral confirms these assumptions. The *Jornal Diário de Notícias,* for example, published the following account in an article entitled "Vagrants and Troublemakers":

> On the 15th November Square, at the corner of the Historical Institute [Piedade] and the intersection with St. Francisco [church], gather daily individuals of both sexes: weight laborers, fruit sellers, and others who are just unemployed or drunkards, displaying a debauched excessive language.
>
> The capoeiragem among men, and the gossiping among women are an "obligatory daily show" with no consideration to the persons who pass through, namely, mothers and children. Police authorities from the Sé [square], making patrols will have to do something and hunt these deranged elements of society. (*Jornal Diário de Notícias* 1911)

Adriana Albert Dias offers another example of capoeira practitioner involvement in street brawls with the police. It is the story of Pedro Porreta, a famous troublemaker, who among other things was also a capoeira practitioner. In the narrative, Porreta is subdued by armed policemen in the streets for causing disorder in public (Dias 2006: 34). Dias considers that Pedro Porreta and Pedro Mineiro were two of the most infamous capoeira practitioners before 1930. Both were known for being skillful capoeira players as well as violent troublemakers. Police deemed Mineiro a vagrant and a petty thief who used to cause a lot of troubles around bars in the center of Salvador; he was someone who constantly got into troubles with whomever crossed his path (Dias 2004: 69). Pedro Porreta was also a dangerous troublemaker. He was particularly a nuisance to the police. According to Josivaldo Pires de Oliveira (2005: 68), Porreta is one of the most often remembered capoeira practitioners today because of his troubles with the police and his demise at a police station in 1914.[2]

Nowadays, popular capoeira songs refer to Pedro Mineiro's death and to his fame as a troublemaker, including the following:

Torpedo battleship from Piaui
armored in Bahia
absolute sailor
arrived provoking fights
They killed Pedro Mineiro
inside the police office.[3]

Women also appear in connection with capoeira in this period. Prostitutes and other female workers formed part of the quotidian life of the streets. Waldeloir Rego was one of the first academics who identified a specific woman connected to capoeira; her name was Salomé, a samba dancer (Rego 1968). However, there is no clear evidence from newspapers that women played capoeira in the streets (Oliveira and Leal 2009). The books written by Pastinha and Noronha do not mention female capoeira players in the *roda,* although they note their presence around capoeira in the roles of wives, sisters, lovers, or troublemakers.

Perhaps the most famous woman of this period in the context of capoeira, apart from Salomé, is Francisca Albino dos Santos, also known as Chicão. Francisca was a troublemaker who, according to Oliveira and Leal, was also in charge of a famous brothel in Salvador. She used to get into trouble with police and capoeira practitioners, and probably knew some capoeira skills herself (Oliveira and Leal 2009: 130–31).

The violent perception of capoeira during 1866–1930 suggests that this practice belonged to the marginal underworld of Bahia. Capoeira was marginal not only in the sense of its political-economical connotations, but also in its social classification. It was an activity for the excluded, for those who lived at the limits of social acceptability such as blacks, rogues, pimps, tough guys, lower-class workers, and vagrants. This description of capoeira as a marginal activity offers significant parallelisms with other dance practices. For instance, Eduardo Archetti highlighted the male-centered urban position of tango as well as its origins, which were derived from marginal forms of dance expression like the Cuban habanera, the *milonga,* and the Afro-Uruguayan Candombe (Archetti and Dyck 2003: 222). Unlike capoeira, tango experienced a rapid expansion and popularity both in Argentina and in Europe as early as 1910, due to its seductive and erotic appeal (ibid.: 223). Capoeira, on the other hand, did not experience wide acceptance internationally until the 1960s, and it never acquired a high status in its local context until the end of the twentieth century.

From the Streets to Institutionalization: Mestre Bimba and the Luta Regional Baiana

A movement formed by middle-class intellectuals and highly ranked military officials brought General Getulio Vargas into power in the revolution of 1930, which abruptly ended the old regime of the First Republic. With Vargas's arrival to power, a new political era was initiated in Brazil; this era has been denominated by historians as the Estado Novo (New State) and could be characterized as a dictatorial regime that combined the positivist ideologies of the period with military coerciveness and a fervent, pristine nationalism. This led to a "tropical" variant of European fascism, according to Antonio Risério (2004: 484). Vargas and his followers had in mind the modernization and unity of the country. His appeal to a "new Brazil" and a new national identity included a series of policies that would have serious repercussions for the next generation of Brazilians. Capoeira could not escape this situation, although its practitioners did benefit from the New State's aim to create a national identity.

The main capoeira figure in this period was, without question, Manoel Dos Reis Machado, who was known as Mestre Bimba[4] (1900–1974). Bimba is considered by many *mestres* today to be responsible for the institutionalization of capoeira in the 1930s. His role is of such importance that many of the subsequent transformations in capoeira during the twentieth century were, in part, echoes of his innovative system. Because this book focuses on the perceptions of the *mestres,* this discussion will stress the influence he had among his contemporary *mestres* and how he determined that institutionalization was the best path for capoeira.

According to Brazilian intellectual Jair Moura, Mestre Bimba was born in 1900 in the area of Engenho Velho (Moura 1991: 24). Luis Renato Vieira (1996) mentions that Bimba learned capoeira from an African called Bentinho at the age of thirteen. Bimba was a big man, almost two meters tall, and dexterous in the art of capoeira. In his youth, he joined street gangs and was considered a tough guy; he gained fame and reputation as a capoeira practitioner during festivals and in the improvised gatherings that often occurred outside bars and nightclubs (Assunção

2005: 132; Rego 1968: 35–36). Some argued that he was originally an *angoleiro*[5] (a person who practices capoeira Angola) who could beat anyone in the improvised street gatherings.

Bimba was influenced by other existing martial arts currently popular in Brazil, like jujitsu and karate. He introduced substantial changes to capoeira around 1930. For him, capoeira lacked effectiveness as a system of self-defense, and provided a serious disadvantage to practitioners when they were challenged by those who knew other martial arts. Therefore, he included new bodily techniques and formalized many of the existing rules concerning the combination of attacks and counterattack sequences. This fact marked the modernization of capoeira, a resignification that strived to transform it from a marginal activity into a sportive, combative practice.

One of Bimba's main influences was Aníbal Burlamáqui, who was also a capoeira practitioner. Burlamáqui was born and raised in Rio de Janeiro. He was an athlete with experience in weight lifting, gymnastics, and boxing (Assunção 2005: 130; Burlamáqui 1928; Pires 2002). Burlamáqui's project was to make capoeira a sportive activity. He wanted to modernize it and transform it into the national sport par excellence of the new regime. He said that this could be possible only if capoeira instructors were able to include different methods of training in their teachings, like the use of weight lifting, boxing, jujitsu, gymnastics, and other martial arts techniques. He was sure that his system of training would make of a capoeira practitioner the most efficient of athletes. Burlamáqui was, without question, a pioneer in developing the sportive approach to capoeira.

According to Frederico de Abreu, Bimba was aware of the small pamphlet Burlamáqui had made to promote his approach to capoeira, and he was familiar with the existence of other martial arts (Abreu 1999). He began teaching in 1918 and opened his academy in Salvador in 1930. According to Mestre Decanio (Decanio 2001a) (one of Bimba's oldest students still alive at the time of my research), it was José Sisnando Lima, a medical student, who brought to Bimba the idea of opening a capoeira school. Bimba accepted this opportunity, and opened his academy under the label of Luta Regional Baiana (Bahian regional fight, now simply called Capoeira Regional). He could not name it *capoeira*, because the Brazilian penal code still considered capoeira to be an illegal activity. Sisnando, being from an upper-class family, had connections with the politicians of the period, and helped introduce Bimba to the governor, Juracy Magalhães, in the early 1930s (Decanio 2001a: 34).

Bimba's brief incursion into the high spheres of power brought him the opportunity to influence the current policies related to the prohibition of capoeira. He received from the Secretaria da Educação, Saúde e Assistência Pública (Bahian Department of Education, Health and Social Security) a diploma that authorized him to run his Luta Regional Baiana under the title of "physical education instructor" (Assunção 2005: 141; Rego 1968: 282–283). This fact symbolized, in part, the end of the era of repression for capoeira, and marked its acceptance by the New State. The penal code law was removed later in 1936, and the government gave legal access to the practice of capoeira in Brazil. In time, capoeira would finally gain recognition among authorities as a national symbol of Brazil.

In 1934 Bimba reached out to a recently created Bahian middle class. Bimba taught capoeira to medical students who had persuaded him to open his own academy: "Doctor Rui Gouveia told me that the teacher [Bimba] was interested in talking with them [the students]. He wanted to learn the meaning of the words they said, and he grasped those words and used them during training. The students explained to him the problem of marginality. Then he decided, when he opened his academy, that there was not going to be space for vagrants. He would only accept workers and students" (Itapoan, quoted in Vieira 1996: 137). In order to progress as a martial art, capoeira needed to sever its ties to its ignominious marginal past. In Bimba's academy, there was no room for idlers, troublemakers, and vagrants, and he was very strict in this respect. According to Mestre Itapoan, Bimba was very keen to keep his capoeira style from becoming a marginalized stereotype; when an individual arrived at his academy, the first thing Bimba asked was if that person was a student or a worker. If the individual in question failed to give proof of identity, he was dismissed immediately, with Bimba shouting, "No vagrants here, please!" (Itapoan, quoted in Vieira 1996: 145). The ID requirement put into place a restriction and selectiveness about the eligibility of his students.

In this way, the Luta Regional Baiana was designed for the middle and upper classes in Salvador (Talmon-Chvaicer 2008: 123). Some intellectuals argue that, in order to gain social recognition, Bimba decided not to prioritize the inclusion of the black population in his academy. This was not to say that he was directly banning Afro-Brazilians, although few of them could fulfill the socioeconomic criteria he imposed. In some intellectual circles, Bimba was considered to be a teacher who had sold his capoeira to a white elite (Assunção, 2005: 141). For him, however, it was part of a project of depuration and creation of a new style. Some of the norms of conduct he implemented fomented a sportive attitude into his students; he demanded moderation in the consumption of alcohol and tobacco and a fierce self-discipline. At the core of these restrictions, we see another example of his attempts to overcome the bad reputation of capoeira in society.

Among the specific rules Bimba introduced into his new style was an initial test that indicated the adequacy of a student for the physical demands of capoeira training. According to Renato Vieira, beginners needed to provide physical dexterity, strength, and resistance. During their first class, Bimba ordered the neophytes to perform basic movements, such as a defensive squat, a backbend, or a headstand. Bimba also implemented a test called the *gravata* (neck hold), which consisted of strangling the student either with a neck hold maneuver or with a tie. If the student endured the strangle test without complaining and showed physical strength, then Bimba would accept him as a student (Vieira 1996: 144).

After the initial test, the student underwent a militaristic style of intensive training for at least six months, although this could extend to one year if necessary. During this period, Bimba taught physical movements and techniques of self-defense. He systematized his method in eight sequences performed in pairs. Old students helped the new ones to master the sequences, while Bimba supervised (Vieira 1996: 150). After a student learned the eight sequences, he was allowed to play in the *roda*.

Bimba also designed another method of self-defense called *movimentos de cintura desprezada* (movements of displaced waist). The moves consisted of grappling sequences executed in pairs; their intent was to help the students defend against adversaries of other martial arts in situations of attacks using their hands. After one year of intensive training, students took exams that marked their graduation at the academy.

On graduation day, Bimba would give an opening speech, followed by a talk about the importance of the event. Then, advanced students would play with beginners. They performed the eight sequences and the displaced waist movements. After the movements were executed, Bimba selected a woman, called *madrinha* (godmother) or *mãe* (mother), to give a special medal and a neckerchief to the beginner (Assunção 2005: 139). Bimba usually selected women belonging to his Afro-Brazilian religious group or the student's mother or girlfriend. The neckerchief, which the student had to tie around his neck, symbolized his new status. Bimba explained that the silk neckerchief could protect the student from knife or razor blade attacks, which were a common event among other capoeira practitioners in the streets.

Every year, a new graduation took place in a ritual that Bimba called *batizado* (baptism). The *batizado* consisted of exams where students showed their dexterity in the eight sequences taught by Bimba.[6] The end of the graduation ceremony consisted of a final test where an advanced student had to take the medal off a new graduate using only capoeira movements. If the new graduate could resist the attack without losing his medal, then Bimba acknowledged his new status (Almeida 1986; Vieira 1996: 160).

In every *batizado*, students received new neckerchiefs that represented their ascension in the hierarchy of Bimba's academy (Rego 1968: 286, quoted in Vieira 1996: 159). There were three basic stages in the hierarchy of Mestre Bimba: initial student, graduated, and graduated with specialization. The specialization program included self-defense tactics for dangerous situations in the street. This training included one-to-one fights, simultaneous attacks against two or more opponents, and fights against armed adversaries.[7] After completing the specialized training stage, the student became a "real" capoeira practitioner.

While there are periodic exams and changes in status for students of capoeira, nowadays the specialization rituals and the exchange of neckerchiefs are no longer practiced in Bahia. I found no evidence of Bimba's practices in regional groups.

The *batizados* and ceremonies of initiation were elements that Bimba borrowed from oriental martial arts and adapted to his new capoeira style. Thanks to his efforts, the learning and teaching of capoeira took on a systematic approach that included choreographed movement sequences and extenuating physical training. In this way, Bimba helped to change the perception of capoeira in society. After his method became standardized in Bahia, the capoeira practiced at Luta Regional Baiana was not considered a distraction for vagrants and marginal characters. It became distinct from street capoeira by implementing the practices of a professional and organized martial art, including a strong ritual bias.

By 1935 Mestre Bimba wanted to show that his capoeira method was effective against other martial arts (Downey 2010). Inspired by Burlamáqui's pamphlet, Bimba entered public contests in order to challenge other capoeira players and martial art practitioners (Abreu 1999; Assunção 2005: 133). According to Abreu (personal communication),

Bimba boasted that he could defeat anyone and, in fact, he did![8] He took part in several fights and won all his matches, including, presumably, one against one of the most famous jujitsu fighters at the time. In 1936 the newspapers declared Bimba to be the champion of capoeira in Bahia. All these accounts brought him fame throughout Brazil.

The presence of Bimba in martial arts contests signaled a new chapter in the history of capoeira, as it moved away from the streets and into the sportive arena (Assunção 2014). This change redefined the aims and intentions of capoeira, which clearly were oriented toward the institutionalization of an authentic Brazilian art form. We do not know if Bimba intended to make such a radical transformation, but it seems as though he used the nationalist atmosphere of the time to present his Luta Regional Baiana as a national sport. Bimba's presence in the ring also served to differentiate his style from the capoeira that was played in the streets and public festivities. He professionalized capoeira by creating a systematic method of training (Talmon-Chvaicer 2008: 120).

The method implemented by Bimba became attractive to people who had not been interested in capoeira before. For instance, the Centro de Preparação de Oficiais de Reserva (Training Center for Army Officers in Reserve) hired Bimba to give lessons to soldiers in the Forte Barbalho in Salvador in 1939 (Vieira 1996: 138). Throughout the years, Bimba surrounded himself with influential politicians. Some of his students became teachers and professionals. Some of them moved out of Salvador and started capoeira academies in other cities, including Rio de Janeiro, São Paulo, and Minas Gerais.

In 1953 Bimba performed a demonstration of his capoeira style to the president of the Republic, Getulio Vargas. At the end of the demonstration, Vargas said that capoeira was Brazil's one and only truly national sport (Vieira 1996: 139). This was one of the most significant moments in Bimba's life, one that consolidated his status as a legend among capoeira practitioners.

Toward the end of his life, Bimba felt disappointed at the state's lack of support for his work and began to show his contempt (Assunção 2005: 144, Vieira 1996: 139). In 1973 Bimba moved with his family to Goiânia, expecting to find a better life and continue his capoeira project. However, he died of a stroke in 1974.

Angelo Decanio summarizes Bimba's legacy: "The presence of *mestre* Bimba in the history of Bahia is more important than he being only considered the figure that invented a method to learn capoeira fast. He is the watershed in a period of great personalities of this cultural activity of Bahian origins. ... He is responsible for the evolution, from the artisan learning in the popular *roda* of capoeira to the systematized method of a physical education program. ... Bimba opened the world's eyes to Afro-Brazilian cultural manifestations" (Decanio 2001a: 34–35).

The Creation of Capoeira Angola

The institutionalization of capoeira brought significant changes to the practice and produced a wide diversity of reactions. Bimba's Luta Regional Baiana focused on effectiveness and combative techniques, which begot a substantial amount of criticism. Intellectuals like novelist Jorge Amado, ethnographer Waldeloir Rego, painter Carybé, and folklorist Edison Carneiro disapproved of Bimba's capoeira categorically. They argued that the Luta Regional Baiana had neglected its Afro-Brazilian roots, had lost its essence, and had sold its authenticity to the city's governing elites. This criticism emerged as part of an alternative political project that pursued and demanded a more profound understanding of the black influence in Bahian society.

During the 1930s, within the left-wing intellectuality of Bahia, there was a vigorous attempt to reevaluate the African heritage of Brazil. Academics were against the simplified nationalist version of Vargas's regime, and became its sharpest critics. Famous personalities like the artists cited above, as well as others like Arthur Ramos, Donald Pierson, and Armênio Guedes, together with some of the most prestigious leaders of the Candomblé religious houses in Bahia, formed a unified block that fought for the social acceptance and recognition of Afro-Brazilian culture. The result was a curious intellectual mixture of communism and neo-Africanism (Risério 2004: 501). Of all the intellectuals, Edison Carneiro (1977) was perhaps the most ardent outspoken activist to fight for the rights of Afro-Brazilians. He denounced the social prejudices of the elites against the black population of Bahia and referred often in his writings to the suppression and discrimination of black culture in a city that was 80 percent Afro-Brazilian; he considered this situation inconceivable and intolerable.

In January 1937 Carneiro and Aydano do Couto Ferraz (a journalist strongly committed to the Afro-Brazilian cultural cause) organized the Segundo Congresso Afro-Brasileiro (Second Afro-Brazilian Congress) (Risério 2004: 502), which included representatives from black cultural traditions like Candomblé, samba, and capoeira. The congress successfully brought awareness to the black presence in Salvador and symbolized the beginning of a new path for capoeira by means of introducing a cultural proposition that contrasted in ideals and attitudes with the newborn Luta Regional Baiana created by Bimba.

According to Assunção, the capoeira presented in the congress was defined by Edison Carneiro to be Angola style (Assunção 2005: 151). Carneiro invited some of the most prominent practitioners of capoeira to the event, including Samoel Querido de Deus, Aberrê, Onça Preta, Barbosa, and Juvenal. The aim of the presentation was to show the original and traditional capoeira played in the streets in an effort to destigmatize its association with vagrancy and criminality.

The origin of the name "Angola" still needs further research. It is not clear if it was something that Carneiro pronounced spontaneously, in the rush of the moment, or if it was part of a plan that represented the views of capoeira players. In this sense, there are still some questions concerning why we call it capoeira Angola. Furthermore, it is still unknown whether that name was proposed from an intellectual or some other sphere.

Frederico de Abreu (personal communication) has pointed out the possibility of tracking down the name Angola from the repertoire of capoeira music. He said that it is possible that capoeira practitioners used the name before Carneiro's announcement. Some songs from the beginning of the twentieth century, he told me, refer to the town of Luanda, the capital of Angola. This could mean that practitioners already had a vision of the African influence in capoeira, or at least were aware of an African past transmitted by myths and oral tradition. If this is the case, then it is necessary to consider reevaluating the contents and the persistence of some elements that practitioners might have used as a form of cultural adscription—elements that also shaped the views of the intellectuals who publicly gave voice to this inquiry.

After the Second Afro-Brazilian Congress, there were large numbers of capoeira practitioners who began to call themselves *angoleiros*. These were persons who did not agree with the ideals of the Luta Regional Baiana. Among them were Mestres Noronha, Amorzinho, Vicente Pastinha, Waldemar da Paixão, Aberrê, and Samuel Querido de Deus. Vicente Pastinha was one of the most prominent of these charismatic capoeira practitioners of the Angola style. If we consider Bimba to be the innovator of capoeira due to his creation of the Luta Regional Baiana, then we could consider Pastinha to be the reformer of capoeira Angola. He codified the Angola style and redefined its aims by seeing it as both a bodily art and a philosophy of life. He also theorized about and reflected on it. In fact, he was one of the first capoeira practitioners to put on paper his ideas about capoeira Angola. He also recorded an LP of capoeira music, which was an aspect that he always considered essential in his teachings.

The Founding *Mestres* of Capoeira Angola in Bahia

The epic history of capoeira Angola in Bahia focuses on the influence and agency of charismatic individuals. It is a narrative that shows a historical consciousness of cultural resistance and adaptation to change. Many of the common views that current practitioners of capoeira in general have about their history tend to divide it categorically between the Luta Regional Baiana created by Bimba and the capoeira Angola style codified by Pastinha. However, it is important to mention that the development of both styles benefited from other personalities, as influential as Pastinha and Bimba, who must also be credited for the institutionalization of capoeira. I include in this section not only information about Pastinha, but also data about the other capoeira players who constructed and developed the Angola style from 1940 to 1968.

Vicente Ferreira Pastinha was born in Salvador, on 5 April 1889 (Assunção 2005: 152). He learned capoeira to defend himself from bigger kids and, allegedly, trained with an African called Benedito around 1899–1900. The son of a Spaniard, José Pastiña, and a local woman from Bahia, Maria Eugenia Ferreira (Assunção, 2005: 149), Pastinha was a fragile boy who learned capoeira to defend himself against stronger boys. In an interview, Pastinha described how he learned capoeira:

> My life as a kid was a little bit bitter. ... I found a rival, a kid who was my rival. We engaged in fights, we fought, and I took always a beating, the worst part. In the window of a house, there was an African observing my fight with that kid. Then, when the beating ended, the African called me: "My son, my son, come here!" I came closer to the window and then he said to me: "You cannot fight against that kid, that kid is more astute that you. That kid is a *malandro* [rogue], and you cannot fight against him. ... You want to fight but you cannot. The time you waste getting beaten is better to spend it here at my home." I accepted the invitation of the old man and he taught me capoeira. "*Ginga* [swing] here, *ginga* there! Fall! Stand up!" he used to say. When he saw I was in a condition to challenge the other kid, he said to me:

"Now you can fight against that kid." (Pastinha, quoted in Muricy 1998: My transcription)

Pastinha stated that an African initiated him into capoeira, although historians and researchers have not found information about this African man. The recurrent references to Africa among *mestres* relate to specific cosmological conceptions that will be discussed in chapter 4. For the time being, it is enough to say that both Pastinha and Bimba claimed to be introduced into capoeira by "authentic" African men.

Pastinha worked in the navy until 1910, where he learned Swedish gymnastics, how to play music, and how to use knives for self-defense (Assunção 2005: 153). For the next two decades, Mestre Pastinha became involved in the traditional capoeira performed in the streets, where he gained fame as a good player and a tough guy. Among his epic stories of that time is the one in which he gave a good beating to the infamous Pedro Porreta in a capoeira *roda*. However, despite the numerous rumors about the prowess of Pastinha at the time, there is little information about his presence in the capoeira scene during the 1930s. Angelo Decanio believes that Pastinha was inactive from 1913 until 1941, when he reappeared on the public scene by founding the CECA, which was the first formal academy of the Angola style (Decanio 2001b: 89).

Pastinha's academy opened just when different practitioners of street capoeira had refused to take part in the mainstream development of the Luta Regional Baiana. According to Mestre Noronha, practitioners like Amorzinho, Geraldo Chapeleiro, Onça Preta, Juvenal, and Aberrê (who was, apparently, Pastinha's student) began to refer themselves as *angoleiros* in an effort to differentiate their capoeira from the one developed by Bimba (Coutinho 1993: 17; Assunção 2005: 154). They held a capoeira street *roda* in the Liberdade neighborhood, and they were organized into a very informal academy or institution without a proper name. There were around twenty-two teachers in total.

According to the oral tradition, Aberrê brought Pastinha to Liberdade, and the skills of Mestre Pastinha were of such high quality that he surprised all the other teachers. He was skinny and fragile looking, but his speed and dexterity of movements impressed the other practitioners. Amorzinho, who was responsible for the *roda*, gave Pastinha its command and proclaimed him the leader of the new movement (Assunção 2005: 155; Pastinha 1996: 5; Talmon-Chvaicer 2008: 125).

The CECA struggled from 1941 until 1949 due to Pastinha's unfruitful efforts to reconcile conflicts between himself and those teachers who did not accept his authority. The initial difficulty of institutionalizing the Angola style was due to the reticence of practitioners who did not agree with the idea of moving capoeira away from the streets and into closed places. Despite these ongoing problems, the CECA remained the only and most representative capoeira Angola academy at the time. It included Pastinha's students and other young and famous capoeira practitioners, like Canjiquinha and Gato (Pastinha 1996: 6).

Pastinha systematized the Angola style in five ways. The first was that he organized a formal structure for the music ensemble, which included eight instruments, and outlined a particular way to sing songs. The second was his implementation of a black and yellow uniform, which paid homage to his favorite football team, the Ypiranga. The third way of systemizing the Angola style was dividing the teachers of his academy into seven commissions: of field, of songs, of music, of training, of archive, and of finance, as well as a *contramestre* (the *mestre's* second in command) (Pastinha 1996: 4). The fourth way was his emphasizing a more aesthetic and artistic approach to capoeira, which privileged a feigned attitude in practice over open physical contact. Finally, he introduced philosophical and ethical values into capoeira.

If Bimba brought a sportive philosophy to his Luta Regional Baiana, Pastinha instilled a deep reflection about his art at the spiritual level. Phrases like "Capoeira is malice, is *mandinga,* it is all that the mouth can eat" and, "Capoeira is not violence—it is art, dance, culture, and deception" became hallmarks of his vision about the Angola style. These phrases have persisted until the present. Throughout his life, Pastinha reflected about many issues, including education, capoeira, society, death, and spirituality, and always in a way that was cryptic and full of mystical references. He wrote a book that was published, and also left behind a series of manuscripts that were published after his death. Pastinha considered himself an educator, and his attitude toward capoeira, as described in his manuscripts, was similar to that of a missionary toward his faith. For example, he wrote, "I always had in mind that capoeira needed a generous instructor; with my presence, I designed a destiny to capoeira for the future" (Pastinha 1996: 1).

Although the group faced numerous problems and conflicts, the Angola variant of Pastinha was very popular, and the CECA enjoyed a golden age during the 1950s. In 1953 Pastinha's academy relocated to Pelourinho, in the historical center of Salvador. A new set of students appeared during this period, among them João Pequeno (João Pereira dos Santos, 1917–2011) and João Grande (João Oliveira dos Santos, born in 1926). This new generation of Angola players brought a steady support to Pastinha's vision of capoeira. His charisma helped Pastinha's students to understand the principles of respect, education, refinement, and preservation of the inner rules of the game in opposition to the attitudes of capoeira practitioners playing in the streets. His teachings emphasized the importance of the figure of the *mestre* as a possessor of knowledge and as the main guide and formal authority in the academy. If Pastinha was not the first practitioner to stress the importance of learning with a teacher (Bimba had done it previously), he was responsible for wrapping the figure of the *mestre* with an almost sacred veil. Under Pastinha, learning with a *mestre* meant learning the secrets of the Angola tradition from an authentic source.

Despite the popularity of Pastinha and Bimba, other capoeira Angola practitioners neither followed the rules established by the CECA nor adhered to the Regional style. Of these practitioners, Waldemar da Paixão (Mestre Waldemar 1914–1990), Rafael Alves França (Mestre Cobrinha Verde 1908–1982), and Washington Bruno da Silva (Mestre Canjiquinha 1924–1993) were the most important. They were public figures who played a prominent role in the constitution and consolidation of the Angola style (Magalhães 2011: 73–81).

Although slightly overshadowed by Pastinha, historians like Frederico de Abreu regard Mestre Waldemar as one of the most artistic and skillful capoeira Angola practitioners of his time; he was a key figure in understanding the artistic side of capoeira during the 1940s and 1950s. He held a *roda* in the *barracão* (shed) in his backyard every Sunday. There, he unofficially opened a small capoeira school that was supported by Mestre Traira. In Waldemar's *barracão,* the most famous capoeira players of the time joined and played together in memorable *rodas* (Abreu 2002). Waldemar, who always considered himself more a capoeira musician than an active capoeira player, commanded the *roda* with his virtuous voice.[9]

Waldemar tried to keep his *rodas* open to all kinds of capoeira players, no matter their styles, and his *rodas* were especially attractive during carnival and city festivities. In a video interview with Mestre Itapoan in 1988, Waldemar mentioned that the *rodas* at his *barracão* capoeira were very different from what we see today—they were violent and for tough guys.

Itapoan: Is there much difference between the old times when you played capoeira, and the present?

Waldemar: There is not much difference, but in the past the main difference was that capoeira was used to beat up people. Capoeira was very sinister: the ones who played capoeira were only tough guys, brave men who had the courage to fight. They used knives. (Itapoan 1988)

The association of capoeira with violence in the 1940s and 1950s was a recurrent aspect that haunted the Angola style. On the one hand, old habits persisted, exhibiting the ambiguity of the practitioners' moral attitudes. On the other hand, *mestres* like Pastinha tried to establish a set of values and principles for capoeira Angola.

Mestre Canjiquinha shared a similar view to that of Waldemar concerning violence and aggression. He described the early period of capoeira Angola as marked by recurrent violence: "When I was young, people performed capoeira only on Sundays or in the festivities of the Largo, Boa Viagem, Ribeira, and Lapinha. ... In those times, there existed real capoeira players, tough guys that fought with five or six at the same time" (Canjiquinha, quoted in Vieira 1996: 100). Mestre Cobrinha Verde never had an academy, but he tried to keep a *roda* every Saturday in his neighborhood of Chame-Chame, and occasionally taught in a school. He supposedly learned capoeira in Santo Amaro da Purificação (a city located in the interior of Bahia) with Besouro, who was one of the mythical figures in capoeira history—a man who presumably had a strong religious connection with the Afro-Brazilian religion of Candomblé. Rumors had it that he could transform himself into a beetle and had a pact of invulnerability with his *orixás* (deities).[10] "Besouro, my *mestre,* began to teach me capoeira when I was four years old. ... In that period, he taught capoeira hidden from police, because police persecuted a lot. When he was very angry and police arrived to close the class, he sent us home and he alone beat up police" (Santos 1990: 12). Cobrinha Verde, Waldemar, Canjiquinha, and other teachers like Caiçara, Espino Remoso, Toto de Maré, Traira, and Bigodinho maintained an ambiguous relationship with the CECA (Magalhães 2011: 77–81). While Pastinha exerted a strong influence on these other mestres, they felt overshadowed by his presence. Pastinha had access to the Bahian intellectual circles and he was a good friend of the famous writer Jorge Amado (Morefield 2008), while the other teachers did not have such a prestigious network. He worked full time with capoeira, while the rest had to do other activities in order to support themselves. This unequal situation resulted in rivalries between Pastinha and the rest of the Angola players; none of them was fond of Pastinha, and they expressed their disagreement openly to him. Some even questioned his status as a *mestre,* and these included Cobrinha Verde and Caiçara (Itapoan 1990; Santos 1990: 18). Other *mestres* negotiated with Pastinha, like Canjiquinha, who accepted his offer of a position of authority within the hierarchy of the CECA.

During the 1950s and 1960s, the development of capoeira Angola had in Pastinha its best representative. His new academy in Pelourinho gained attention from local authorities and the tourist office. He held performances in Salvador and traveled with his students to other cities in Brazil, including Porto Alegre, Belo Horizonte, and Rio de Janeiro. In this way, he presented his capoeira Angola as a national folklore spectacle (Assunção 2005: 165).

However, Pastinha's major achievement came in 1966, when the minister of culture invited him and some of his students to the First World Festival of Black Arts in Dakar, Senegal (Assunção 2005: 166). This event signaled Mestre Pastinha's peak of popularity and success.[11] From 1966 onwards, capoeira Angola experienced several organizational problems, which brought as a consequence a declining presence in Bahian society—so much so that the style was almost extinct by 1979.

Facing Extinction

During the 1960s and 1970s, the national capoeira scene changed drastically. On the one hand, it saw the astronomic popularity and expansion of the Luta Regional Baiana (now simply called capoeira Regional). On the other hand, it saw the diminished and faded presence of capoeira Angola academies. The success of capoeira Regional included a new kind of student who expanded Bimba's system to other cities and social classes, transforming it and adding new meanings to the objectives of capoeira. Bimba graduated around fifty students during his lifetime, and at least half of them became *mestres.* As I mentioned before, some moved to other cities and opened academies wherever they went, while others stayed in Salvador and continued working with Bimba. On a national scale, the success of the Regional style caused an increase in the number of teachers and academies all over the country. One of the most important groups during the 1970s was the Grupo Senzala (Senzala Group) in Rio de Janeiro, which had some of Bimba's students among their ranks (Capoeira 2003).

Folkloric ballet companies played a very important role for capoeira practitioners at that time, because these companies hired many of these practitioners as performers, bringing a source of income and assisting in the diffusion of capoeira abroad. Although many teachers refused to take part in the "exoticism" of capoeira promoted by choreographers, the existence of dance companies interested in capoeira brought about new economic opportunities to capoeira *mestres*. Thanks to the interest of dance academies, it was possible to show capoeira abroad in the late 1960s and early 1970s.

The national and international popularity of capoeira Regional had a tremendous negative affect on the Angola style. Pastinha and the CECA fought for a place in the public scene through the 1960s. They did not succeed in gaining the attention of Bahian cultural elites. The decline of capoeira Angola during the following years was in part due to the increasing popularity of capoeira Regional and to the aging of the Angola *mestres*. By 1966 Pastinha was already seventy-eight years old and almost blind. Waldemar, Canjiquinha, and Cobrinha Verde were over forty-five years of age. Their *rodas* had become more irregular because of lack of support. Other teachers stopped practicing capoeira completely in order to work in different occupations. Therefore, the responsibility for keeping the Angola style alive resided mainly in the hands of just a few capoeira practitioners—Pastinha's students who, by this time, were also in their thirties and forties. Among these students, Mestre João Pequeno and Mestre João Grande became the most representative capoeira Angola players of the 1970s. They helped Pastinha to keep his academy alive and motivated the rest of the Angola practitioners to continue practicing and organizing *rodas* despite the practice's clear struggle for survival (Moura 2005: 1).

The near absence of a new generation of practitioners of capoeira Angola at the beginning of the 1970s in Salvador contrasted with the development of capoeira Regional, which had a prolific and rejuvenated group of practitioners who resignified the legacy left by Mestre Bimba. The generational gap between styles produced a distorted and stereotyped vision of capoeira Angola. In newspapers, capoeira Angola was portrayed as a residual practice of bygone times—an archaic version of physical movement no longer used in the mainstream capoeira scene (Assunção 2005: 186). Although always covered with the sacred halo of tradition, the founding Angola *mestres* were considered passive individuals who could be summoned to give prestige and status to the *batizados* of capoeira Regional, but whose age did not permit them to show their skills and full potential against sportive young players interested in competition and effectiveness. Many Angola *mestres* like Canjiquinha,

Bobó, and Waldemar negotiated with the Regional groups. This negotiation was essential for their survival in a threatening environment. They started to use to their position as caretakers of a genuine tradition in order to create a space for a more consensual vision of capoeira that would include elements of both styles in one modern version (Silva 1989: 21–22).

In some academies that were under the influence of Bimba (like Cordão de Oro, Abolição, and Cativeiro), a modern version of capoeira took place during the 1970s. *Mestres* started teaching capoeira Angola and Regional techniques indistinctly in their schools in an attempt to overcome the differences between the two styles. They gave this capoeira the name of Contemporary. Although these classes were very attractive for some capoeira practitioners, particularly in Rio de Janeiro and São Paulo, the new style did not succeed completely within traditional Angola and Regional groups in Salvador. Regional academies like Filhos de Bimba (Bimba's sons) refused to take part in the dissipation of style differences and instead remained loyal to Bimba's teachings and rituals. In the case of capoeira Angola, the CECA remained unchanged in its commitments until the early 1970s, when Pastinha lost his academy in Pelourinho. At the time, he claimed that a rebuilding process was going to take place in the academy and the shut-down was only temporary, but this rebuilding never happened (Assunção 2005: 163; Talmon-Chvaicer 2008: 126). Pastinha, poor and blind, retired to a very discreet life, surrounded by misery and relying solely on scarce support from his friends and students. The artist Carybé and writer Jorge Amado arranged a very small pension for Pastinha, which was only enough to cover his most basic living expenses. He lived in a shelter during the last years of his life, forgotten by the government that once helped him to create his academy.

By 1975 almost all the Angola *mestres* had stopped teaching and ceased to have *rodas,* while those who continued being active, like Canjiquinha, Gato, and Cobrinha Verde, adhered to the new, modern vision of capoeira Contemporary and helped many groups to understand the foundations of the Angola style. Only João Pequeno continued exclusively teaching capoeira Angola to a reduced number of students at the CECA. João Grande, who was experiencing financial difficulties, stopped playing capoeira; he went to work during the day in a gas station and moonlighted as a bus driver in the evenings. Despite efforts made by individuals who were involved constantly in the preservation of capoeira Angola (like Jair Moura, who made a short documentary about capoeira in Bahia in 1968 showing João Grande and João Pequeno playing in the streets), the Angola style experienced a severe decline.

The *mestres'* advanced age definitely played an important role in the decline of capoeira Angola in Bahia. However, the style was not quite so threatened by extinction as history would have us believe. Young practitioners were still reinventing capoeira in the streets, particularly in public festivals. The fact that folkloric ballets included Angola players as part of their shows is also a proof of the practice's continuing presence. This period saw a decline in participation at Angola academies, but not of practitioners of capoeira Angola in general. The shutting down of the CECA in Pelourinho brought a movement of the art into secrecy and a return to a marginal position in society. For those who did not give concessions to capoeira Regional, like João Pequeno and João Grande, survival implied finding new students who could continue their tradition. To succeed by means of institutionalization was not an option in the late 1970s, and the presence and popularity of capoeira Regional deterred any attempt by the Angola *mestres* to keep academies as a profitable activity.

Despite its current problems, João Pequeno took on the responsibility of the CECA and continued teaching. Unfortunately, I do not have information about the location and the form in which the CECA continued from 1974 to 1978. We know that João Grande also worked with the choreographic group Viva Bahia as a player of capoeira music from 1974 to 1978 (Assunção 2005: 186; Moura 2005: 2).

The inclusion of capoeira Angola teachings within new, contemporary groups that focused on removing the distinctions of capoeira label could have marked the end of capoeira differentiation and the end of true capoeira Angola. However, a surprising transformation took place in 1980. Together with Mestre João Pequeno, a young practitioner named Pedro Moraes Trinidade (born 1950) would revitalize capoeira Angola with his mesmerizing way of practicing capoeira, his gifted music skills, and his knowledge of Afro-Brazilian culture.

Mestre Moraes and the revitalization of modern capoeira Angola in Bahia

Pedro Moraes Trinidade started learning capoeira with João Pequeno and João Grande at CECA at the age of eight. Although no information referring to him during the period 1958–1974 is available in journals, there is a photograph of him as a child playing one of the instruments at CECA in 1958. The young age of Moraes's commencement of study was unusual among capoeira practitioners at the time. João Pequeno, Cobrinha Verde, Waldemar, and Caiçara learned capoeira when they were teenagers, whereas João Grande did not start until he was twenty.

Moraes was one of the few practitioners who remained active during the declining period of capoeira Angola. He also had the opportunity to meet other great capoeira practitioners, like Mestre Nô, who was famous among capoeira Contemporary circles in the 1970s. Moraes stated that he learned exclusively from João Grande and considered himself to be a follower of Pastinha's tradition and a supporter of CECA's ideology.

Pedro Moraes moved to Rio de Janeiro in 1973. He worked in the navy and, at the same time, held a job as a guard at a metro station. His arrival to Rio de Janeiro coincided with an increasing popularity of capoeira Regional and capoeira Contemporary groups in the city. Jair Moura, Matthias Assunção, and some of Moraes's old students point out that this expansion played a significant role in the way Moraes began to conceive of capoeira Angola. For him, capoeira Angola meant a commitment with an Afro-Brazilian tradition in ways that did not allow much innovation and experimentation with other styles. Moraes viewed capoeira Angola as a holistic practice constituted by many parts, including fighting, musical skills, rituals, self-discipline, inner philosophy, political awareness, and spiritual growth. He made these aspects explicit:

> The capoeira player, who is attentive to the art he practices, knows how to transport his knowledge acquired symbolically in the *roda* of capoeira to the big *roda* of life. He knows how to behave, he knows when is the right moment to go forth, and when is the right moment to run away. It is an apprenticeship, by the way, very difficult, and probably with no end. These intrinsic principles of capoeira are the milestones of its life philosophy, and a fundamental part of its existence. ... The process of apprenticeship is not limited to the mastering of kicks and movements, it includes all the totality of being. (Moraes, quoted in GCAP and ACANNE 1989: 37).

Moraes was young, skillful, and eager to show what he had learned in Bahia, so it is no surprise that there is a rich set of stories surrounding the personality of Mestre Moraes. Between the years 1973 and 1979, the young Moraes participated in Regional *rodas* in Rio de Janeiro. He played hard, fast, aggressively, and yet acrobatically. He combined physical skills with a vast musical knowledge and expertise in form. According to some of his old students, Moraes liked to defy other capoeira practitioners in public events as part of his plan to revitalize and transform the Angola style. His performance showed to other practitioners that the stereotyped perception of capoeira Angola as something for old people was wrong.

He began giving lessons in 1974, and he founded the GCAP in Rio de Janeiro in 1980. This period was crucial for the enactment of Moraes's objectives. Capoeira Angola was only known in Rio de Janeiro as it had been taught within the capoeira Contemporary groups, in bits and pieces. Moraes considered the fusion of styles to be misleading, however, because it distorted the meaning of capoeira Angola as a holistic, unique practice. His posture was radical concerning the mixing up of styles. He strongly rejected any attempt to combine Angola, Regional, and Contemporary styles under a unified form labeled *capoeira*.

The GCAP attracted the attention of many carioca (inhabitants from Rio de Janeiro) practitioners, who saw in Moraes's charisma and personality a source of inspiration, according to Mestre Cobra Mansa (personal communication). He showed to these initial students that capoeira Angola could encompass all the attributes of the Regional style but remain loyal to the traditional values predicated by Mestre Pastinha.

The GCAP in Rio successfully produced a new generation of eager young students who followed Moraes's precepts and were interested in the situation of capoeira in Bahia. Moraes would not move to his hometown until 1982; until then he remained in Rio, working and consolidating his academy.

On 5 February 1981 in Salvador, Bahia, Mestre Pastinha died, abandoned by society and in complete misery. Following Pastinha's death, many practitioners in Bahia foreshadowed the death of the Angola style. However, João Pequeno, aged sixty-three, continued teaching capoeira at the Forte Santo Antônio Além do Carmo, which by then was almost falling to pieces. By the end of 1981, there were no more than three or four Angola academies in Salvador, all of them struggling for survival and clearly at a disadvantage against the Regional and Contemporary academies. In 1982 Mestre Cobrinha Verde died, and again voices raised among practitioners of capoeira Regional claimed that capoeira Angola was extinct. During this crucial period, Moraes decides to return to Salvador to support Mestre João Pequeno. Talking about the situation of capoeira Angola in Salvador in 1982, Moraes mentions the following: "At that time, capoeira Angola was agonizing due to the death of *Mestre* Pastinha, and also due to the pressure of capoeira Regional, which was still hegemonic; it was a hegemony nourished by the discourse elaborated by its practitioners who were always interested in showing capoeira Angola as an art for the illiterate, without meaning in a sociopolitical context (Moraes 2000: 12). Mestre João Pequeno welcomed Moraes back to Salvador and let him teach at CECA in the Forte Santo Antônio. For one year Moraes worked together with his old teacher to plan the structure of the GCAP. He officially opened his academy in the Forte Santo Antônio, in the upper level of the building, in 1983. From this moment on Moraes would spread his vision of capoeira Angola, in part by bringing back together all the retired Angola teachers. "When I returned from Rio to Salvador I decided to reunite the *mestres* of this art, who were presented at the time only as museum pieces, through capoeira Angola workshops promoted by the GCAP. I invited them to create together a movement in support of the return of capoeira Angola, something that I would not have achieved without their direct participation (Moraes 2000: 12). In 1985 Moraes organized the Primeira Oficina de Capoeira Angola (First Workshop of Capoeira Angola) in Bahia, in which the majority of the old teachers participated with their students (Magalhães 2011: 113). He also invited Mestre João Grande to teach at the GCAP. Gradually, the Angola style gained more popularity among the younger generation of practitioners, and more people became interested in the cultural foundations of capoeira Angola.

During the early 1980s the GCAP and the CECA were the most important academies in Salvador. The revival of the Angola style motivated many teachers, including Mestres Curió Caiçara, Bola Sete, Zé do Lenço, Jorge Satélite, Virgilio, Roberval, Bobó, Pelé, and Lua de Bobó, to open their own academies. Slowly, capoeira Angola began to gain terrain in the general capoeira scene.[12] Many of the academies in Salvador opened branches in other cities of Brazil. The GCAP continued in Rio, but inaugurated another academy in Belo Horizonte. Canjiquinha graduated a significant number of students in Brazil, some of whose practice was similar to the Angola tradition. These mestres included Paulo dos Anjos, Ananias, Lua Rasta, and Brasília.

In fewer than ten years, a new generation of Angola players arose in Salvador. Headed by the charismatic personalities of *mestres* like Curió, João Pequeno, and Moraes, the art form of capoeira Angola experienced a rebirth in the city of Salvador. This meant also a continuity of the philosophies of Pastinha, Cobrinha Verde, Waldemar, and Canjiquinha.

Of all the academies, the GCAP was one of the most rigid. Mestre Moraes structured his academy around a set of obligations and a level of control, and supervision that had an almost military aspect. This gained him the reputation of being a polemical and controlling figure. He was also one of the first Angola teachers to incorporate the ideology of African revivalism, and he posited this ideology at the core of his teachings.

The stereotypical perception of a capoeira practitioner was of one who was somewhat roguish, disorganized, and without formal education. Moraes did not match the stereotype at all. He studied law at university, earned a master's in history, and learned English as a second language. The discipline he introduced in the GCAP included an emphasis on the importance of education and self-growth among his students. For most of his close students, Moraes was not only a *mestre,* but also an educator, a mentor, and a family member.

In fifteen years Bahia's GCAP had graduated one *mestre* and six *contramestres.* The first and only teacher formed by Moraes in this period in GCAP Bahia was Sinésio Feliciano Peçanha (Mestre Cobrinha Mansa, born 1962). Cobrinha Mansa worked closely with Moraes as an important member of the GCAP until his departure to Washington, D. C. in 1994, where he established the FICA together with Mestre Jurandir, another of Moraes's students from Rio de Janeiro. Three of the *contramestres,* Valmir Damaceno (Valmir, born 1965), Pepeu (Moraes's son, born 1970), and Poloca (birth year unknown) obtained their titles in 1990; they trained with Moraes during the 1980s and part of the 1990s. Marcelo Conceição dos Santos (Boca do Rio, born 1970) became *contramestre* in 1993, and continued being part of the GCAP until 1996.

Two female capoeira practitioners, Paula Barreto (Paulinha) and Rosangela Araújo (Janja) graduated as *contramestras* (the female form of *contramestres*) in 1994. Their graduation indicates the gradual acceptance of female leaders within Angola groups and the beginning of a more gender-inclusive perspective of capoeira. Capoeira Angola was a male activity until the 1980s, when Moraes and other *mestres* began accepting women in their trainings. The graduation of two female players as *contramestras* in 1994 was therefore a significant achievement. It made possible the creation of groups led exclusively by women, as Janja and Paulinha both eventually achieved the title of *mestra* (the female form of *mestre*).

The year 1993 was a turbulent period of conflicts and rivalries among capoeira Angola *mestres.* The possibility of unifying the Angola academies in Bahia into a unique federation, like some old *mestres* wanted, seemed like a dream. Moraes and the GCAP did not want to negotiate with Regional groups and with the Angola teachers who liked to combine styles; other *mestres* like Curió, João Pequeno, Renê, and Virgílio believed that there was no hope of bringing everybody together, and instead decided to focus on their own personal projects.

By 1996 all the former *contramestres* from GCAP, excepting Pepeu, had left the group for various reasons and had created their own academies. This process helped to extend the influence of capoeira Angola groups in Salvador (Zonzon 2007: 6–8). Valmir joined Cobrinha Mansa at FICA; Janja, Paulinha, and Poloca created Grupo Nzinga, which had locations in Salvador, Brasília, and São Paulo; Boca do Rio formed Grupo Zimba in 1996. Moraes never forgave the departure of his outstanding students, and his relationship with them deteriorated, although in recent years he seems to have reconciled with some.

Global Trends

The number of practitioners of capoeira Angola in Bahia has increased notably in the past twenty years, thanks to the opening of the above-mentioned academies and to the continuation of previously existing Angola groups. João Pequeno, who died in December 2011, graduated some of the most important teachers of the past two decades, including Jogo de Dentro, Pé de Chumbo, Faisca, and Ciro. Mestre Curió also graduated his wife Jararaca as a teacher, making her the first female Angola *mestra* in Salvador (according to him). Curió graduated three other remarkable students: Augusto, Marcelo, and Gafanhoto. Mestre Roberval, the leader of the Grupo Filhos de Angola (Group Sons of Angola), graduated two young *contramestres*: Gato Preto and Pezão. This proliferation of a new generation of young capoeira practitioners ensured the preservation of the Angola style for the future. This revitalization was the result of a huge effort made by several charismatic personalities who had dedicated their lives to the project of diffusing capoeira.

In the new millennium the number of Angola academies in Salvador has increased notably, from three academies registered in 1982 to more than twenty in 2015. This is a good recovery for the style, although the number of capoeira Angola academies is small compared to the fifty or more existing Regional academies in the city. In a general sense, capoeira Angola is still a marginal practice in Salvador.

However, the relative success of capoeira Angola brought along its increasing exposure to an international audience, which resulted in a growing global interest, particularly among Europeans and Americans.

In the 1990s the international appeal of capoeira Angola inspired two of its biggest *mestres* to leave Brazil. João Grande moved to New York in 1992 and Cobrinha Mansa began a nomadic existence in 1994. He has practically lived on planes because of his travels from one country to another. Nowadays, it is common for every Angola *mestre* in Bahia to maintain a close relationship with groups in Europe, the United States, and Latin America, and to travel abroad at least two or three times a year. In some cases, *mestres* have opted to live a life of seasonal migrations, living abroad for some periods of the year and then returning to Bahia for the rest of the year. There are also *mestres* who live overseas and return to Salvador only for short periods during a calendar year.[13]

Migration and mobility is an issue and adds a layer of complexity to the social configuration of Bahia. It has also brought new market opportunities for capoeira. There are foreign capoeira students who wish to train with the "living legends" of the "traditional" style and "drink from their fountain of wisdom," as one of my international capoeira friends told me. Traveling to Bahia has become an "apprenticeship pilgrimage," according to Lauren Griffith (2016), who aptly described the incessant desire of players to visit the "mecca of capoeira" at least once in their lifetimes. In this sense, the role played by tourism is changing the capoeira scene by providing a new, lucrative business for *mestres*. At the same time, the presence of female foreign capoeira players has instigated substantial debates about the democratization of the art and the public acceptance of the presence of women in Bahian capoeira hierarchies. The proliferation of new technologies like the Internet and social networks has also made capoeira Angola an international and globally accessible practice.

I cannot predict how these global transformations will affect the dynamics of the interaction of *mestres* and academies in Bahia, but I venture so far as to say that the external influences will not completely determine the future development of capoeira Angola. On the contrary, I believe that charismatic and powerful individuals will continue to play an important role due to the demands of the international markets and the competition that *mestres* have among themselves. My guess is that the cause of social and historical transformation will always pass through *mestres'* decisions, actions, and influence. We can thus safely assume that *mestres* will try to keep their tradition close to their own historical experience and dynamics of power. However, it is also possible that capoeira Angola will soon become something completely different from what we see now. If this is the case, I am sure that the change will depend on the agency of individual actions and decisions and the motivation of *mestres* to adapt to a changing world.

Notes

1. This is similar to what Eugenio Soares (2001) found in Rio de Janeiro during the nineteenth century, where capoeira practitioners had diverse ethnicities and socioeconomic backgrounds.
2. The death of Mineiro is recounted in detail in the diary of Mestre Noronha (Coutinho 1993: 24), and is mentioned by Assunção (2005: 121) and Dias (2004: 65).
3. Torpedeira Piauí
   Couraçado in Bahia
   Marinheiro absoluto
   Chego pintado arrelia
   Matarão Pedro Mineiro
   Dentro da Secretaria.
4. He is supposed to have gotten his nickname at birth, when his mother lost a bet with Bimba's midwife; the mother was sure it was going to be a girl, but when the midwife saw it was a boy, she exclaimed in a loud voice, "Bimba!" (which means "little penis" in Portuguese.) I thank Mestres Nenel and Frede Abreu for providing this detail of Bimba's story.
5. The idea that Bimba was an *angoleiro* is debatable, since there is no record of capoeira Angola before 1930, according to Matthias Assunção (2005).
6. According to Bimba's son, Nenel, *batizados* are still widely performed globally in capoeira Regional groups nowadays, although with modifications and new meanings.
7. For a more detailed description of the capoeira Regional ritual, see Assunção (2005: 137–39).
8. For a detailed account of Bimba's prowess in the ring, see Abreu (1999).
9. In the photographic archive of Pierre Verger, one can appreciate some of the memorable moments of the *rodas* at the *barracão* during the 1940s and 1950s.
10. For a description of the myth of Besouro see Pires (2002).
11. The popularity of Pastinha in Salvador was enhanced by his position not only as a *mestre* but also as a philosopher of capoeira and an artist. In this respect, he was different from other *mestres,* who did not possess that cultural capital. Perhaps this was due to Pastinha's artistic predisposition as a painter and musician. As Pastinha embraced capoeira Angola's African heritage as one of its foundational principles, this heritage gained the support of many Bahian intellectuals, particularly of Jorge Amado who, in some of his books, mentioned the importance of Pastinha as an important figure in the preservation of authentic Afro-Brazilian traditions. I believe that

Pastinha's capacity to dialogue with other intellectuals about race, philosophy, and art was one of the reasons he was considered a true bearer of an authentic form of capoeira. This is perhaps why he and his group were chosen to participate in the First World Festival of Black Arts in Senegal.

12. This does not mean that there were no conflicts between Moraes and other *mestres*. In fact, there were and still are many problems related to Moraes's personality and the way he presents his role as the savior of capoeira Angola in Bahia. Many *mestres* have tried recently to minimize the importance of Moraes in the modern history of the Angola style and have talked openly against his influence and his "distorted" way of presenting facts.

13. There is an increasing bibliography on the global expression of capoeira, which has expanded to include many different disciplines, approaches, and locations. Although the following list is by no means exhaustive, I invite any reader interested in the international development of capoeira as a practice to consult the following references: Aceti 2013; Delamont 2006; Delamont and Stephens 2007, 2008; González Varela 2012b; Guizardi 2011; Hedegard 2012; Joseph 2008, 2012; Robitaille 2014; Rosario, Stephens, and Delamont 2010; and Stephens and Delamont 2009.

CHAPTER 2

✤ Capoeira Angola in Its Own Right

In this chapter I describe the practice of capoeira Angola as constituting a world in itself, from an ethnographic perspective. I consider that *mestres* are not only agents of historical change, but also are responsible for the way relations exist among capoeira practitioners today. As Bruno Latour mentioned, social scientists often abuse the word "social" as an absolute and controlling term (Latour 2005) that describes any kind of relations between humans. He says that the anthropologist should not take the so-called social for granted as something already defined prior to any human interaction. The analyst's commitment should be quite the opposite: to trace associations in order to configure the social. In this sense, the social is what needs to be explained rather than something that is already influencing actors.

Although this book is not framed under the theoretical standpoint of the Actor–Network Theory, I consider the method of tracing associations as a good and viable starting point to describing the way *mestres* constitute the social as a result of their own agency and a consequence of their power. As I have shown in chapter 1, groups have flourished in Bahia since the revival of capoeira Angola in the 1980s. Transformations have occurred through the actions of charismatic persons. *Mestres* established relationships as a form of keeping control of their modes of interaction and expression with others. They insist that they will never forget the marginal and endangered position that capoeira Angola experienced during most of the twentieth century. However, the success of Angola academies in the past twenty-five years has inspired a set of relationships very different from those established by *mestres* of the past. Capoeira Angola is more popular now than it was in the past, and is usually played indoors. This has also created new relations among practitioners in Salvador. These new relations have evolved into what *mestres* call the capoeira Angola community (CAC).

The CAC is characterized not by political or economic grounds, but by its provision of an identity to *mestres* and a sense of belonging to a certain tradition. In this sense, the CAC comprises a set of relations that *mestres* build in their process of sharing and transmitting knowledge. These relations locate and organize powerful individuals in lineages, or lines of knowledge, as the *mestres* say, that legitimate their status and position as men of power. Thereby, the CAC becomes the underlying principle that gives consistency and validation to the hierarchical relations that exist at the interior of the Angola groups.

Ultimately, the notion of *community* emerges from the historical and epic accounts of the *mestres* discussed in chapter 1. Paradoxically, the CAC is both a result of historical interrelations with external forces and influences and a product of the *mestres* themselves. The CAC is shaped in the image of the leaders; it is the consequence of their own experience of learning capoeira with older and wiser *mestres*. In other words, the institution of the CAC acts as a mirror image of the *mestres'* power.

Delimiting a World in Itself: Differences between Capoeira Angola and Capoeira Regional

The definition of capoeira Angola depends on its differences from other capoeira styles. As I have shown before, there was a time when capoeira in Bahia was divided into two kinds: Angola and Regional. This division established an asymmetry between both styles, causing antagonisms and rivalries that still exist today. This section describes the aspects in which the styles differ. It attempts to justify the existence of capoeira Angola as a unique holistic configuration that refuses to create a common unifying perspective among all capoeira variants.

From the point of view of Angola practitioners, an amalgamation of styles is unimaginable. But why is this the case? The first tentative answer has to do with a distinctive conception of power held by practitioners of capoeira Angola, and with the style's difference in the way it treats the body and magic. The second main difference is that Angola and Regional stand in an asymmetrical relation concerning their mutual influences in society. Regional outnumbers Angola in the number of practitioners and academies in the city, as well as in visibility in the media and in Bahian mass culture. The Angola style, which is situated in a relatively marginal position compared to Regional groups, has used this disadvantage to claim a closer involvement with African traditions, thereby perpetuating the idea that the style maintains a purer connection with its origins that has not yet been contaminated by the external influences of mainstream sports or other martial arts. Thus, the creation of the CAC can be understood as an attempt to close the practice of capoeira Angola to external influences.

What makes capoeira Angola different from the other existing styles in practice depends on who defines it. I could not find one clear narrative among practitioners that established the essential differences objectively, nor did I discover a general consensus concerning the definition. Many of the simplified explanations coming from Regional practitioners, such as "Regional is acrobatic, Angola is not," and "Angola is traditional, Regional is sportive" do not always correspond to reality, and could lead to misinterpretations and misunderstandings about both practices. Because many of the assumptions about styles vary depending on who is explaining them, one sometimes feels tempted to skip the problem, adducing that the dilemma is irresolvable. Nevertheless, a separation exists, and there is a clear opposition between Angola and Regional, and also between Angola and the more recent Contemporary style (Merrel 2005; Reis 2000).

The division is still prevalent due to an internal recognition, identification, and differentiation of practice. Since it is impossible to take a position of pure objectivity in this debate, I make my starting point the perspective of the Angola *mestres,* with the main purpose to gain understanding of why they think their practice is unique and in what sense they think it is different from the Regional style.

Dress Code

The dress of the Angola style practitioners is one of the easiest ways to identify them from the Regional practitioners. Angola players normally dress in a tucked T-shirt with the logo of their group, a pair of trousers, and shoes. The colors of the clothes vary and there is not a single standard uniform. Some Angola groups prefer to use the combination of a yellow T-shirt and black trousers, which was popularized by Mestre Pastinha's academy. Others prefer to use all white clothes; all black clothes, as was used in the academy of Mestre Bola Sete; or all of any other color. The most important aspect of dress in the Angola style is not so much the color of the clothes, but the use of shoes. According to a conventional rule in the Angola groups in Bahia, a true *angoleiro* never plays barefooted. Additionally, an Angola player always needs to tuck his T-shirt into his pants; playing topless is unthinkable, unless one is performing in the street, where wearing a uniform is not essential.

Because the system of hierarchies in Angola does not require differentiation in the player's clothes, there is nothing distinctive in the garments that could be used to infer the status of a participant. The Regional and Contemporary groups, on the other hand, adopted the system of ropes created by Mestre Bimba; during events, they wear these distinctive items in order to identify themselves according to their different stages of learning. Regional and Contemporary groups can play either with shoes or without shoes and their clothes can look more sportive; for instance, women sometimes are allowed to wear tank tops, while men are allowed to wear sleeveless T-shirts or to play barechested.

Bodily Movements, Music, and Songs

Nowadays, many Contemporary and Regional groups include Angola movements as part of their teachings. Therefore, it has become very difficult to sustain a formal distinction based on the kicks, attacks, and counterattacks of each style. Many Contemporary groups start their performances playing Angola, in a slow rhythm and close to the ground, sustaining long interactions. Then they speed up the pace to a full intensity that includes summersaults, and very short games. Regardless of this, Angola practitioners hold that the way a player's body moves in a *roda* will indicate whether he is really from the Angola tradition or not. They say that true capoeira Angola players have smooth, loose movements with no rigid *ginga,* and that they maintain a protected body while doing acrobatic moves. In Angola, players can play up or down and remain always relaxed, smiling, and in complete control of their bodies. They deceive their opponents by displaying theatrical moves and strategies that disguise their real intentions. *Mestres* argue that a true Angola practitioner will not try to do summersaults or acrobatic moves in the air without his hands. They say that a practitioner needs to be in contact with the ground at all times, and always be prepared to execute a counterattack.

Nowadays, ethnographic data contest the oppositions traditionally used by famous Regional teachers and some academic books to define the capoeira styles (see Merrel 2005: 11–17). These oppositions include assertions such as that there is a slow game in Angola and a fast game in Regional and that there is less violence in Angola and more violence in Regional. Both styles include fast and slow games, violent and non-violent situations. In this sense, from the Angola practitioners' point of view, the difference in the styles seems to reside not in the intensity or the speed of the game, but in the way they perceive movements (especially the *ginga*) to be rigid or loose, and whether acrobatic moves, like cartwheels and handstands, are opened or closed.

Angola *mestres* mention that they could never imagine singing songs that refer to Regional *mestres* like Bimba or to Contemporary groups like Abadá or Senzala; however, Contemporary groups are happy to sing Angola songs, and their repertoire also includes its steady rhythms, while Regional groups try to stick to Bimba's traditional songs and music. They always use two or three basic, steady rhythms in their live performances. However, mutual musical influences exist among the different styles, despite of the reticence of Angola practitioners to adopt songs written about capoeira Regional. Angola players have adopted some of Bimba's rhythmic music styles, although they do not use them very often during performances. Still, many Angola *mestres* profess a respect for the work of Mestre Bimba. They think that he was not only an excellent player but also a great musician who contributed to the diffusion of capoeira to a wider audience. Their criticism of the Regional style is not directed to Bimba, but to some Regional groups and the way they have departed from their true Regional roots.

Loyalty to One Style

One of the main differences between capoeira Angola and the other two capoeira styles has to do with loyalty to style. For instance, Angola practitioners will refrain from imitating Regional or Contemporary moves while playing and say that a true Angola practitioner will never take lessons with a Regional teacher. Angola *mestres* do not mind playing against Regional opponents, but they will never pretend to play like them. My informants often stated that, once you have been initiated in the Angola style, you should stay there. The reasoning behind this advice is that it is impossible to master both variants. For instance, Mestre Moraes told me once that he had been training Angola for more than fifty years, and he was still learning and trying to understand it. Therefore, he said, how could he believe in the expertise of persons who advertised that they were teaching Angola and Regional in their academies? "I think that all my years of training were pointless," he said sarcastically. "I will have to change and learn from those men, because they are in a higher level than me; they are teachers of Angola and Regional, and they are only thirty years old. I will definitely start taking lessons with them."

In this sense, many Angola teachers in Salvador establish a distinction between what they conceive as authentic capoeira Angola, and the "Angonal," which they mockingly describe as a bad imitation of Angola performed by Contemporary groups.

Representation of Knowledge and Experience

One of the most significant differences between capoeira Angola and capoeira Regional resides in the way they symbolize the transmission of knowledge. Regional groups normally have *batizados* once or twice a year in order to change degrees in the hierarchies of the group. Regional academies have many branches in Brazil and abroad, which attract a substantial number of practitioners in their national and international events.

Batizados are special occasions that provide recognition and change of status. This change offers an incentive to the gradual development of students of capoeira Regional because it modifies their position in the hierarchy. At the same time, a *batizado* motivates students to pursue a more committed involvement in capoeira, because doing so will increase their ability and dexterity; it also symbolizes a new status with more responsibilities and obligations. Some academies have a system of ten to fifteen stages, symbolized by the use of ropes, before the title of *mestre* can be achieved. Others have fewer or more stages, depending on their individual structures. As Janja, an Angola *mestra*, wrote,

> Sportive capoeira became more popular, and focused internationally. Through *batizados* groups coordinated by young mestres, contramestres, professors, graduated students, and players reproduced quickly, which give them *legal* [emphasis in original] grounds to graduate new students. Competition and tournament rules substituted initiation practices and rituals. Imitating the traditional clothes used in oriental

martial arts (judo and karate), the official outfit of capoeira became a white uniform with a rope tied to the waist.

On the contrary, the few who remained associated with the capoeira Angola tradition re-orientate it [capoeira Angola], in the best possible way, toward the market and consumption of symbolic goods. Discourses assumed, overwhelmingly, the character of black resistance. (Araújo 1999: 34–35)

The Angola style has never included *batizados* or the use of ropes as a way of representing knowledge. These are elements that contradict the precepts of tradition. On the contrary, *mestres* of capoeira Angola do not hold regular initiation ceremonies. For them, knowledge is the product of the relationship between a student and his *mestre*. There are few titles in capoeira Angola: *mestre, contramestre,* professor, or *treinel*.[1] The way that a student achieves these titles is not standardized, but depends arbitrarily on each *mestre's* decision. A student may train with a *mestre* for several years without obtaining any reward or recognition. Only a few will receive the title of *mestre*. The majority will never pass the barrier of student, professor, or *treinel* in their lifetimes. The symbolization of knowledge in capoeira Angola is thus very different and much more limited than in capoeira Regional. It takes a long time to gain recognition in capoeira Angola and there are no immediate rewards. In this sense, a student must gain experience and invest time in order to see whether he can improve his status.

The external, visual aspects of difference among styles have a strong impact in the way capoeira Angola and capoeira Regional are perceived socially in Bahia. Some capoeira Regional practitioners and Angola players characterize Regional exclusively as a martial art or sportive practice. It is advertised in fitness centers, martial arts academies, and dance institutes. Sometimes, capoeira Regional professors and teachers are involved in the practice of other martial arts or in the local fitness culture; in some cases, practitioners use their dexterity and flexibility in shows or public performances. Because of their plasticity and their visual spectacle, there are a wide range of marketing options for Contemporary and Regional groups. This gives them a social advantage over capoeira Angola, because they can reach a larger, more diversified audience.

The harshest critics of capoeira Angola tend to be orthodox Regional *mestres*. They characterize the style as inflexible and reluctant to change, despite calls for its adaptation to the demands of contemporary society. They sometimes consider capoeira Angola to be marginal, intransigent, and outdated. This might be another reason that Angola cannot contend with capoeira Regional in its social impact, number of adepts, and diffusion.

However, the Angola style is viewed by practitioners of capoeira Contemporary as a complementary practice that provides the basis of an old tradition; they view it as a form that one must learn, adapt, and perform in order to understand capoeira. According to Mestre Nestor Capoeira, "Later—years later—the *Capoeirista* gets the urge to enrich his or her game with aspects that have nothing to do with techniques or kicks but rather with the ritual of the game. There comes the urge to learn the aspects of *Angola*. ... If it does not happen, the player can paint himself into a corner, and the game of capoeira can turn into a physical dispute, dull and frustrating" (Capoeira 2003: 139). It is common to find that *mestres* of capoeira Regional or capoeira Contemporary assume themselves to be Angola experts. They argue that all an Angola practitioner needs to know is how to perform capoeira close to the ground with slow movements. When I asked a famous Regional *mestre* about his opinion concerning the differences between styles, he replied, "Regional? I am not a Regional—my *mestre* was Nô, and he was an *angoleiro*. Therefore, I am an Angola player, too, and I teach Angola in my academy. I play both styles and I am a *mestre* of both capoeiras."

Although many of the detractors of capoeira Angola are in part right in their criticism of the reluctance to change of the style, the marginal position of capoeira Angola is partially due to causes other than its lack of adaptation to modernity. The marginality of Angola academies is an act of preserving tradition. Angola groups do not participate in sportive or martial art capoeira projects because they consider them to be inauthentic forms of expression. Before the advent of social media and the Internet, Angola academies had no clear advertisements outside their spaces. This was due in part to a conscious decision made by *mestres* to remain detached from the increasing global commercialization of capoeira and the interest in Afro-Brazilian culture as an exotic representation of the Other. Because *mestres* refused to consider capoeira Angola as a sport or a spectacle, they purposefully declined visibility and remained marginal compared to other capoeira styles.

Today, the Internet has changed dramatically the way capoeira Angola is presented to the world. Instead of trying to compete with their Regional or Contemporary counterparts in a sportive fashion, Angola *mestres* focus on art and culture as forms of channeling their message of tradition. Although Angola practitioners prefer to consider their capoeira to be a philosophy of life and a never-ending process of apprenticeship that cannot be devalued or diminished by the demands of the market, they consider their legacy to be finding its right promotion in artistic and creative arenas. Many *mestres* are reluctant to be considered as sell-outs by focusing just on money and profit, or by commercializing with Afro-Brazilian tradition.

Capoeira Angola *mestres* are dedicated to follow a strict commitment to the legitimate use of their tradition, so aspects that seem to contradict these dictates are emphatically condemned. This fact has had, as a consequence, a shared perspective in which capoeira Angola is classified as the "mother of capoeiras," or the most traditional one (Almeida et al. 2013: 1350). Chapters 3 and 4 will describe in detail what is meant by the term "tradition" and what elements of capoeira Angola displays cannot be found in other styles. The next section will describe the elements and interrelations of the Angola community in Salvador.

Preserving Tradition in a Changing Landscape

Salvador is a city of geographical, racial, and economic contrast. The central area located in the upper city and known as Pelourinho is a historical district currently designed almost exclusively for tourists. From there, several slopes bring you to the lower city, where banks and markets operate during work days. The magnificent Elevador Lacerda connects *cidade baixa* and *cidade alta* (the lower and upper cities,[2] respectively). Salvador, Bahia, thus has a diversity of geographical and social landscapes that include deep cultural contradictions.

The difference between the upper and lower city could serve as a metaphor for the struggles for social inclusion, which is a dilemma that has not found a clear solution in Salvador. Bahia is predominantly Afro-Brazilian; historian Antonio Risério estimates that more than 80 percent of the population are Afro descendants (Risério 2004).

Salvador was the first city founded by Europeans in what it is now known as Brazil. It became the capital of the Portuguese empire in the New World in 1549 and retained that central administrative position until 1711. Since its foundation, the city was the port of entrance for a flood of commercial and cultural influences from Portugal and its African colonies (Silva 1994). This New Lisbon, as many Portuguese called Salvador in the sixteenth and seventeenth centuries, became the main point of commerce for slaves coming into the territory. It is difficult to estimate the total number of slaves introduced to Bahia during the period of slave trade. Nicolas Parés used official records to calculate that more than 1 million slaves were introduced to the city ports between 1710 and 1850 (Parés 2006: 63–64). However, the number could increase to 2 million or even more because of illegal trade, the inaccuracy of registers, and the number of slaves introduced before 1710. Because of the slave trade, the African presence became more predominant in society and the city's shape changed.

Abolition arrived relatively late in Brazil (1888). If we think of history in terms of processes of long duration, not much time has passed since then—it's been less than 150 years. The weight of history is felt while one roams the city center, when one looks at the historic building and churches, when one pays attention to its religious diversity, and when one's gaze focuses on the Baía de Todos-os-Santos (Bay of All Saints).

The weight of history influences the way capoeira Angola exists in the state of Bahia, too. For many capoeira practitioners around the world, the Bahian Recôncavo (bay area) has become the Mecca of capoeira. Thousands of people all year round visit the region in order to explore its historical and cultural heritage. Many of the visitors view the martial art displays in Salvador and in the Recôncavo as another tourist attraction. Capoeira has been caught in the dynamics of tourism, which has flooded the region.[3] The practice has become increasingly more commercial, and the local authorities have begun to exploit capoeira as a cultural attraction in order to generate more revenue.

As I mentioned in the previous section, the Angola style is in a marginal position compared to the Regional style. Although there are perhaps twenty academies registered (mainly in the historic center and neighboring areas), when I began my research in 2005 I struggled to locate them. Some of them did not bear distinctive signs or labels. Academies did not have updated Web sites and some did not advertise their opening times or training hours. *Mestres* were not interested in advertising their art commercially.

In addition, there were only few places and occasions at which capoeira Angola was performed publicly. Most events were held in closed spaces. This indicates that capoeira Angola academies were not looking for attention and visibility in the local market. *Mestres* seemed more interested in keeping groups small (up to around ten to twenty members), which echoed the early capoeira group configuration and kept them near to what they frequently called their "African roots."

However, the attitudes of detachment and secrecy have slowly been changing, due in part to the increasing demand of tourism, by federal projects like the Forte da Capoeira,[4] by the international expansion of groups via the Internet, and by the travels of *mestres* abroad. The renovation of the Forte has brought many capoeira Angola groups out into the open. The interest of the Brazilian government in promoting the practice of capoeira in general has compelled Angola *mestres* to become more accessible and open to negotiating and discussing issues of visibility and how to financially support their art. The changes brought by the Forte would be a discrete study in itself. Still, despite the new demands of the market, the social existence of capoeira Angola still relies on activities performed inside academies that remain separate from commercial exploitation.[5]

This does not mean that capoeira Angola is a secret cult. *Rodas* are open to everybody, and every academy I visited had chairs in place to accommodate a non-capoeira audience. Nobody is banned from entering an academy unless the person is drunk, smoking, or wants to cause trouble. The Forte has regular *rodas* whose main witnesses are tourists. While past *mestres* were concerned about players from other styles who came to the *rodas* to cause problems or to close an academy through means of violence, today *mestres* encourage people who stand at the entrance of an academy to either come closer to the *roda* or to leave the premises. *Mestres* said that it is still important to pay attention to possible troublemakers whose bad energy (standing in the doorway with arms folded) can impact their academies.

The Capoeira Angola Community

Beyond the influences of the market and at the core of capoeira Angola groups stands the CAC. The CAC was a recurrent term throughout my interviews and the articles and film recordings I reviewed. In the early stages of my research, it was difficult to understand precisely what *mestres* meant by the word "community." My first thought was that they were referring to a kind of formal association or organization created by *mestres* of capoeira Angola. In fact, I found out that there was an association of Brazilian capoeira called the Associação Brasileira de Capoeira Angola (ABCA; Brazilian Association of Capoeira Angola). The association was created in 1991 in order to provide support to old *mestres,* and was designed exclusively as a center for the practice of capoeira Angola. However, I learned later that the ABCA was by no means representative of all the *mestres* and academies of capoeira Angola in the city. As time went on, it became clear that ABCA was just one more organization represented by only a handful of old students of Mestre Pastinha and few other *mestres,* most of whom were advanced in age.

I spoke with two of the most respected capoeira experts, Jair Moura and Frederico de Abreu, about this issue. They told me that there had been an increasing expansion of academies since the Angola revival in 1980, but that attempts to structure the movement had failed. Almost all *mestres* took separate paths; they were negligent of and skeptical about creating a possible union in a wider confederation. Moura and Abreu said that *mestres* were not interested in becoming so institutionalized; some of these *mestres* considered that the path to form an Angolan confederation would bring only troubles, because it might generate power struggles among the academies. Additionally, a structured union would go against the dictates of tradition, which explicitly conceived capoeira Angola as an act of resistance against hegemonic power. Therefore, Moura and Abreu thought that academies should be almost exclusively personal projects. Their idea of a CAC was not of a clear, organized, defined institution.

When I addressed the existence of a CAC with some *mestres,* they told me that the idea of a CAC was based on the feeling of belonging to a common historical identity. Many of them said that the community was formed by all *mestres,* dead and alive, who were connected to the Angola practice in one form or another. They told me that such a community was not necessarily restricted to a geographical area. It encompassed all of the *mestres* dispersed around the world. For instance, one of the pillars of the community was Mestre João Grande, who has lived in New York since the early 1990s. Other *mestres* who have lived abroad for at least ten or fifteen years are also considered by practitioners in Salvador to be essential components of the CAC. The CAC seemed intangible, lacking in exact boundaries and geographic locale. It was a construction based on associations, on lines drawn in an abstract, mental set of relations. In fact, I concluded that the CAC was made up of the *mestres* themselves, and the lines emerging from them.

Based on this logic, one must have established a direct link with a *mestre* in order to belong to the CAC. This is made evident in the lyrics of opening songs, which praise the value of a *mestre* in the process of learning. These lyrics often include phrases like "Long live my *mestre* … he was the one who taught me capoeira."[6] Therefore, we can affirm that the ascription of students to the tutelage of a *mestre,* and their acceptance of his role as an educator in possession of knowledge, is a form of tradition. A student with no association with a *mestre* is left adrift in the world without recognition and guidance. As Morton Marks notes, "Whoever in capoeira doesn't have a master has no 'tradition', no reference point. This is because the master's name functions like a passport in the world of capoeira, and without it, the capoeirista would be a nobody"(Marks, quoted in GCAP 2003: 26).

Another of my friends, Mestre Valmir, talked, in one of our conversations, about the sense of belonging in these terms: "The world of capoeira Angola is small … and we are all in the same ship". In this case, Valmir used the metaphors of "world" and "being in the same ship" intentionally. He believes that a student becomes a member of his *mestre's* tradition by accepting a relationship of apprenticeship with the *mestre*. Therefore, capoeira Angola provides the opportunity to create a different set of social relations around a relatively small number of people, or around a relatively small number of prominent leaders who construct a world in itself. As Mestre Moraes noted, "The world is the *roda* of life" (Moraes quoted in Araújo 1999: 89). Life in the world, for him, is a circle where people face opponents and challenges.

As I researched capoeira I realized that the notion of community could not be disassociated from the role played by the *mestres*. However, I found it difficult to describe the meaning and limits of the term "community," because the word seemed too abstract to be represented empirically. Indeed, students struggled to give a clear definition of it. Beginners even had difficulty grasping the different modes of organization in academies; advanced students also hesitated when they tried to provide a definition of the elements that unite the *angoleiros* in Bahia. Despite these conceptual difficulties, most of the students agreed that the *mestres* should play a central role in the social organization of the community. As many of the interviewed practitioners mentioned, it was not possible to consider a student a true *angoleiro* until he was associated with a *mestre*.

To give a privileged role to the *mestre* raises questions about the social construction of subjects. Do *mestres* embody social relations? Or, as Letícia Vidor de Sousa Reis argues (Reis 2000: 174), are their bodies the embodiment of a social microcosm? These are difficult questions to answer. There is definitely a general social context that cannot be dismissed when one refers to the role, power, and status of a *mestre*. The forces of Bahian society and its history influence many of the social relations at the interior of capoeira. However, aspects of race discrimination and the economic class divide are challenged within capoeira groups and are actually contested by the *mestres*. In this sense, *mestres* do not want to reproduce in their academies what is happening in their lives outside capoeira. The CAC is the *mestres'* answer to the racial and social conflicts they experience in the city as Afro-Brazilians. It is their reaction against mainstream society, rather than an identification with it. Similarly, the term "*mestre*" is itself a product of history, a concept designed to subvert the dominance of Bahian society over Afro-Brazilians. In that sense, a *mestre* is a figurative inversion produced by social forces in conflict, in part legitimated by other *mestres* and their students (Paiva 2007).

With the revival of capoeira Angola in the 1980s, the role of the *mestre* acquired a new dimension; his importance has increased with time. That the CAC depends nowadays on the figure of these charismatic individuals is, in part, due to the expansion of academies at national and international levels. *Mestres* assumed the responsibility of caretakers of tradition as a form of control over the new global situation of capoeira Angola. The role played by a *mestre* has to do with legitimization, as Mestre Moraes states:

> There exists a very important fact to be observed in Capoeira Angola nowadays: its demographic and geographic expansion. It is necessary to foment the awareness of the capoeira practitioners in this process of expansion with the purpose that capoeira will not be limited only to a way of playing capoeira. When I talk about control or awareness, I do not think about an institution that will determine who can or who cannot practice Capoeira Angola, but to a group of mestres truly recognized, who would have as their main objective to give continuity to the wishes of Mestre Pastinha. (Moraes 2000: 14)

The core of the CAC is formed of *mestres* truly recognized who sanction the inclusion or exclusion of members in the community of practitioners. This principle ensures that a person becomes a man of power by being acknowledged as such by another senior human being, or a group of seniors. This verticality in the hierarchy of knowledge exemplifies how the CAC depends on powerful individuals. In this sense, the CAC is visible when *mestres* meet to initiate practitioners into the higher ranks of the hierarchy. Although there are no specific rules about the characteristics of any initiation in capoeira Angola (actually, the time required to improve one's status varies: it can happen every five, ten, or twenty years), many *mestres* are present to witness and give their approval to a new initiate whenever a person changes status. Mestre

Moraes himself asserts how important it is that *mestres* be present: "The title of mestre, according to Capoeira Angola tradition, is given by the acknowledgement of the community to the person who, besides exercising control and mastery over the game, the singing, and the rhythm of capoeira, also has the capacity to transmit his knowledge to other persons. Using his body, and his word, a mestre guides his disciple into the game of capoeira, and in life" (GCAP and ACANNE 1989: 37). Mestre Valmir, in an informal conversation we had, also stresses how important it is that *mestres* be recognized by others as such to be considered legitimate: "It is not only about the title, nowadays you can even buy it! The important thing is to be acknowledged." One can conclude, therefore, that by creating and justifying a link with a truly recognized *mestre*, a practitioner gains entry into the CAC. This is the only way to do it, and *mestres*—at least those in Bahia—know that they are responsible for the maintenance of a legitimate form of adscription.

On the other hand, the sense of belonging to a common tradition is strongly felt when something unexpected happens among capoeira practitioners. During my stay in Bahia, the teenage son of one of my informants died in a motorbike accident. As a form of tribute, the father, a famous *mestre*, held a *roda* in his son's honor. I took part in the event, which was a kind of funeral where people came to pay their respects by playing capoeira. Many *mestres* were present and brought their students. The wretched father gave a speech at the end of the *roda*. He thanked everybody for coming and mentioned that the best way to say good-bye to his son was by singing and dancing. Finally, he said that it made him happy to see all the members of the CAC present, even those *mestres* whom he had not had the time to meet before. Everybody remained silent and, for a brief moment, all who were present felt that we were part of the same community, people sailing on the same ship.

Lineages

Mestres of capoeira Angola conceive the CAC as an extension of themselves, a collection of the lines of knowledge leading back genealogically to the dead *mestres* and their African ancestors. Most of the *mestres* I interviewed referred to their community metaphorically in terms of lineages. Although they were not related by kinship, *mestres* conceived their relationships with their senior *mestres* to be parental and educational, particularly those *mestres* who had directly mentored them. They used the word "lineage" when talking about their ancestry and tradition.

Based on the information provided by *mestres,* four main lineages make up the CAC, and these lead back to the four founding *mestres* of the Angola style, who are considered nowadays almost as mythical figures: Pastinha, Cobrinha Verde, Waldemar, and Canjiquinha. Any current *mestre* who wishes to be acknowledged and respected as such has to prove a convincing link to one of the four founding *mestres* or to their disciples.

It is at this level that one finds the only relatively consistent structure of the CAC. Lineages make *mestres,* and place them in a series of intricate interrelations that provide the only available representation of the community. Although the lineages are very complex to outsiders, due to their multiple ramifications, they are frequently the object of analysis and reflection for many *mestres.*

Nevertheless, there are individuals who claim to be *mestres* in their own right, without trying to probe any social ascription to a lineage or the CAC. They can create a large following of students without trying to form academies or lineages of their own. Because legitimation is a big issue among the established Angola *mestres,* these marginal individuals are sometimes not considered to be true *mestres.* They are positioned on the fringes of the social relations among Angola academies. However, even in these extreme cases, *mestres* may try to find them a place in the ancestral lineages of the mythical figures of capoeira in order to make them acceptable, whether or not these individuals wish to be included in the lineages. After all, a marginal individual who considers himself a *mestre* may use his position as a "renegade" to criticize the forms of authority imposed by legitimated *mestres,* and refusing any form of categorization would be necessary to maintain this renegade identity.

Pastinha's lineage is often considered to be the most influential and respected, because the most prestigious *mestres* of capoeira Angola in the past twenty-five years claim a direct link to his person. Figure 2.1 depicts the most representative *mestres* who are organized around Vicente Pastinha. Although the diagram is restricted to the *mestres* directly related to Bahia and focused only on João Pequeno's, Curió's, and João Grande's subsequent lines, it shows how *mestres* draw their relations mentally, spatially, and figuratively. Sometimes a lineage ends or dwindles, as in the cases of Cobrinha Verde and Waldemar. Neither of these two *mestres* had a substantial number of disciples, either because their disciples died young or because they switched styles for capoeira

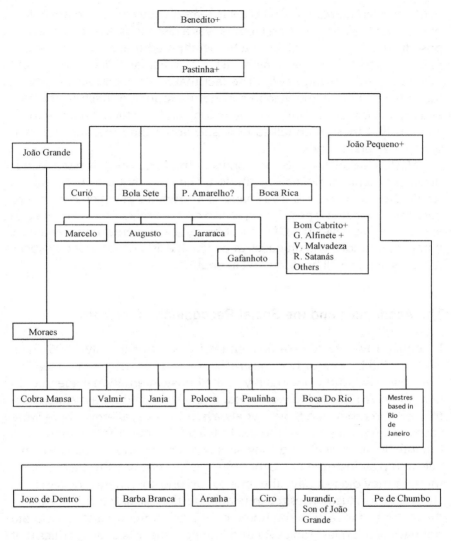

Figure 2.1. The lineage of Mestre Pastinha. Diagram based on the lineages depicted at the FICA Bahia headquarters.

Regional. However, there are still some *mestres* in Bahia who claim to be direct descendants of Cobrinha Verde and Waldemar.

The four founding *mestres* of capoeira Angola learned their art from persons who are difficult to identify. Pastinha claimed to have learned from an African man called Benedito; Waldemar from *mestres* Canário

Pardo and Sirí de Mangue, who disappeared without leaving any information but their names; Canjiquinha was a disciple of Aberrê, who supposedly died in a *roda;* Cobrinha Verde affirmed that he was a disciple of Besouro de Mangangá, a mythical figure in Bahian folklore who could transform into a flying beetle. The fact that it is impossible to identify the initial source of knowledge among the founding *mestres* of capoeira Angola is part of their own mythology and mystery. What we know so far is that these men talked profusely about their *mestres* and their deceptive personalities.

Mestres argue that lineages configure the CAC, which is not a recognized economic or political institution. The lines that *mestres* create in relation to other *mestres* give shape to a structure in which new members can be located. These lineages also create a hierarchy of knowledge and power. However, the CAC is not just an ideal mental representation. It implies attitudes and practices of power. It exists in the scope of social relations, which will be discussed in depth in the next section.

The Academies and the Social Recognition of a *Mestre*

I identified twenty Angola academies in Salvador in July 2006. Each one was led by one or two *mestres,* but not all academies had leaders available year-round, due mainly to their busy international agendas. In fact, some groups had to work most of the time without a *mestre.* Mestres, on the other hand, did not always own an academy. There were cases when *mestres* were too old to teach (like Mestres Bigodinho and Gigante, for instance), and they simply appeared in the *rodas* to sing, talk, and play instruments. Other *mestres* did not want to have academies, or they did not have the time to run one. In general, the situation showed a surplus of *mestres* in relation to the existing academies. The ABCA, for instance, was the home of at least thirteen *mestres* who did not have academies. Tables 2.1 and 2.2 show the lists of academies that I registered, as well as their names, their dates of creation, the *mestre* or *mestres* in charge, and their location. It is not an exhaustive list, and it has left aside some groups that no longer exist or have stopped regular trainings. It also does not cover other branches from the same group in the city; the names given are only those of the headquarters.

Mestres base their relationship on reciprocity. This means that *mestres* and members of an academy should go and visit *rodas* from other groups if they expect to have visitors, too. *Rodas* are the most important

Table 2.1a. Academies in the historic center and neighboring areas of Salvador, Bahia (2010)

Academy and year of its foundation	Mestre or mestres in charge	Location
Grupo de Capoeira Angola Pelourinho (GCAP), 1980	Moraes	Forte Santo Antônio, historic center
Centro Esportivo de Capoeira Angola (CECA), 1978	João Pequeno	Forte Santo Antônio, historic center
Associação Brasileira de Capoeira Angola (ABCA), 1993	Boca Rica, Neco, Pelé da Pomba, etc.	Historic center
Semente de Angola, 1994	Jogo de Dentro	Garcia, 2 km from historic center
Capoeira Angola Irmãos Gêmeos, 1982	Curió	Pelourinho historic center
Fundação Internacional de Capoeira Angola (FICA), 1996	Valmir	Largo dois de Julho, 1 km from historic center
Associação de Capoeira Angola Navio Negreiro (ACANNE), 1985	Renê	Largo dois de Julho, 1 km from the historic center
Centro de Cultura de Capoeira Tradicional Bahiana, 1980	Bola Sete	Vila Velha, 1.5 km from historic center
Associação Capoeira Angola Reliquia Espino Remoso, 1980s	Zé do Lenço	Sete Portas, 1 km from the historic center

events of an academy, especially on Friday, Saturday, and Sunday. It is also common that a *mestre* will pay a visit to other *mestres* on special occasions, such as for birthdays, the anniversaries of groups, or when he wants to advertise an event.

There are around fifty *mestres* currently living in the city of Salvador, Bahia, although not all of them know each other. Due to the constant global mobility of practitioners, sometimes a *mestre* has heard the name of another one but has never met him. On some occasions, the only way they know of a *mestre* is through his past affiliation with an older *mestre*. In spite of their mobility, *mestres* keep track of each other through their students, through sporadic meetings, and through gossip. All of them are globally connected through social networks like Facebook, and many now use this platform to organize their national and international agendas. Therefore, sometimes one finds that *mestres* from Bahia interact more, or get to know each other better, when abroad, because they are brought together in big events in the United States and Europe more often than in their hometowns.

Table 2.1b. Academies in other neighborhoods and in the Ilha Itaparica
(distance more than five kilometers from the historic center)

Academy and year of its foundation	*Mestre* or *mestres* in charge	Location
Grupo Nzinga, 1996	Janja, Paulinha, and Poloca	Rio Vermelho
Grupo Zimba, 1997	Boca do Rio	Pituaçu, Boca do Rio
Filhos de Angola, 1981	Roberval	Pituba
Capoeira Angola Palmares, 1979	Mestre Nô	Boca do Rio
Capoeira Angola Bonfim, 2003	Professor Sinho	Bonfim
Capoeira Angola Mozambique, 1990s	Neco	Brotas
Capoeira Angola Primeiro de Maio, 1980s	Virgilio	Fazenda Grande
Grupo Capoeira Angola Cabula, 1996	Barba Branca	Cabula
Grupo Acupe, 1990s	Marrom	Brotas
Grupo de Capoeira Angola Angoleiros do Mar, 1990s	Marcelo Angola	Ilha de Itaparica
Grupo de Capoeira Angola, Menino de Arembepe	Lua de Bobó	Dique de Tororó

Age and, above all, years of experience secures a *mestre's* place within the hierarchy of the CAC. A practitioner normally becomes a *mestre* when he is forty years old or more, although this depends on the age at which he started capoeira. Perhaps twenty-five years ago, a student could become a *mestre* at a younger age after studying for ten or fifteen years, like Mestre Cobra Mansa, who achieved his title at the age of twenty-four. Nowadays, however, titles are more restrictive and difficult to achieve. The number of capoeira players has increased exponentially, and starting students at a very young age has become a common practice in Bahia. There is a lot of competition among practitioners and there is an unwillingness from *mestres* to give titles unrestrictedly to students even if they have trained for many years.

Sociologically speaking, there are no clear rules defining the procedures and reasons to give the title of *mestre*. Often, it is a matter of dispute and questioning. This is a common concern for any practitioner, and one of the sources of conflicts among *mestres*. Students often make jokes about the name "*mestre*" and sometimes play along with the relativity that this term implies. For instance, they keep calling each other "*mestre*" as a way of teasing, knowing that they will never get a title because the process sometimes seems an almost endless journey.

The best way to avoid conflicts of legitimatization is to present a new *mestre* directly to the *mestres* of the CAC. I witnessed a *mestre* who wanted to give the title to one of his old students. He called many different leaders of academies to a *roda,* where he announced officially that his student was about to become a *mestre.* This act made visible to others that he was personally handing the title to a student. At the same time, he demanded from the others that they address the initiated officially as a *mestre.* The behavior of the assembled *mestres* is one of respect. They agree with the giving of a new title in the ceremony, for the most part. However, in private I have heard disagreement and criticism that someone received the title of *mestre* too early, too fast, or without really deserving it, although I haven't heard of a *mestre* protesting during a ceremony of graduation.

The public announcement of a new leader in front of a group of *mestres* is one of the few occasions where the feeling of belonging to a community seems to be real and concrete. In those special *rodas, mestres* play with each other, which does not happen often in Salvador, because the *mestres* want to avoid power clashes among each other.

Constant interaction among powerful individuals is not desirable. This is one reason why it has been very difficult to form a confederation of capoeira Angola *mestres.* As I have mentioned before, attempts to bring together all leaders under an institutionalized organization have failed due to suspicion, mistrust, envy and personal struggles.

Conflicts and Rivalries

Social relations in capoeira Angola hint at many conflicts and disputes that are normally hidden. The ways *mestres* act are defined by two modalities: personal secrecy and distancing and differential forms of reciprocal visits. Concerning the former, *mestres* learn in their process of apprenticeship that close interaction among them is not possible or desirable. *Mestres* are deceptive individuals who cleverly have developed different strategies to keep their distance from other persons, particularly their students. They will be open, friendly, and talkative to any person up to a certain extent. However, when it comes to power and sharing their personal views about their knowledge, they are more reserved. They might seem to be showing their most intricate skills during a workshop, while truly they are disguising their true knowledge. This attitude becomes more evident throughout the years of interaction that a student builds with a *mestre*. In a sense, this secrecy is a characteristic form of preserving power in a spiritual and religious sense.

The latter modality of differential forms of reciprocal visits complements the idea of personal detachment and closure. Some *mestres* try to visit other academies on special occasions or to make announcements. However, clashes of power and authority are frequent, and dissension in the various magical and religious views of the *mestres* happens recurrently. As Mestre Cobra Mansa said in an interview I had with him during one of his workshops in Salvador, "Sometimes it is difficult [for *mestres* to visit other academies] on account of their ego, and because their personal problems. But this new generation is not having these problems. Thus, Mestre Poloca comes here, I go to his academy, Renê comes here, Valmir goes there. There is more integration now." However, when I suggested to him that reciprocal visits were not a common practice, he said, "Look, this is very simple. You are not going to stop strengthening your own home in order to strengthen others' home. We are busy persons and we must give priority to our own academies. Our students can go anywhere, but we sometimes do not have the time."

Although Mestre Cobra Mansa's remarks were conciliatory and defended the idea of reciprocal visits, he acknowledged to me that those kinds of interactions seldom happened. However, he warned me that the current lack of interest in keeping the links of reciprocity must not be viewed as a problem between academies, but as a problem between *mestres*. They are powerful subjects, and any situation of risk means a challenge to their status and prestige. Some of them are no longer interested in manifesting their capacities and abilities in a *roda*, so they focus attention more on their success in the competitive international market. As Frederico Abreu once told me while we were arguing about the politics in capoeira "*Mestres* are no longer interested in showing to other *mestres* in Bahia that they are good players. Everybody knows it already—the leaders have created their own history, and they have achieved prestige from their former years and from their lineage. If one trained with Pastinha, one has got, in theory, the qualifications automatically."

Today, the value of a true *mestre* appears in the relationship he builds with his students and not through direct confrontation with other *mestres.* Echoing the words of Frederico Abreu, Mestre Nestor Capoeira talks about the process of apprenticeship of a *mestre:*

> You are now a master. There no longer exists any distinction between you and capoeira: you live it; you are one and the same. You now possess the penetrating glance that is able to discern what goes on between two players, not only on the physical level, but also on the mental and spiritual levels. You no longer feel the necessity or the urge to experience this or that new or unknown *roda,* and you no longer feel the need to measure yourself against someone who is said to be a great player. You have been around and have seen the "world go around" again and again, and you have established a network of *camarás* [comrades], young and old players who are spiritually akin to you and whom you meet again and again throughout the world. Or, perhaps as a consequence of the unfriendly acts and attitudes of your youth, you have become a lone wolf in your later years, admired and respected by the young and inexperienced, but avoided by your peers who have no interest in doing any sort of business with you. (Capoeira 2003: 32)

It seems that *mestres* who have achieved a certain level of knowledge have to focus on giving lessons, strengthening their academies, forming new students, and keeping *rodas* regularly to the extent that these duties eclipse their showing of status through participation in the *rodas.* So a differential form of reciprocity among *mestres* seems to be the norm in capoeira Angola. For instance, leaders with more trajectory symbolize and externalize their own personal power by avoiding any kind of reciprocity at all, as in the case of Mestre Moraes, who almost never visits other academies and who often does not allow his students go to other *rodas.* During my time in Bahia he visited the ABCA *roda* only once. Moraes's indifference to building links of reciprocity makes him a difficult person to deal with, as some of his ex-students explained. However, the CAC tolerates and fears him because he is one of the most powerful capoeira players of all times.

Other *mestres* show their consideration to others by appearing occasionally in other academies or in public events as guests. A *mestre* who wants to pay a visit to a *roda* will do so according to his precepts of power and status, measuring the kind of relationship he has with the person in question within the lineages of the CAC. In this sense, a *mestre* is very cautious and selective. He will never tolerate public humiliation in a *roda.* He will never show up in an academy where he is not welcomed or where he does not have any connection at all.

Workshops, Festivals, and Public Gatherings

The organization of seasonal or annual events called *oficinas* (workshops) is another form of reciprocity found among capoeira Angola academies. Workshops are two- to five-day events that are designed to bring students and *mestres* together by fomenting interaction and participation. They include intensive days of training, discussions about capoeira, music lessons, films, and *rodas*. They also attract Brazilian and foreign tourists. On these occasions, the organizers (usually an academy and its national and international branches) advertise the event by distributing flyers among the different capoeira groups in Salvador. In workshops it is common to find famous leaders appearing as special guests. The *mestre* or *mestres* in charge invite other *mestres* to give talks and, in some cases, to impart classes.

Workshops create a system of alliances that help to attenuate conflicts among *mestres* and help form solidarity links. The events also bring money to the academy and the *mestres* who organize them. Because some of these workshops are advertised on the radio and TV, they confer a momentary, social visibility to capoeira Angola. Workshops apparently produce an ephemeral solidarity between the *mestres* and make possible more interactions at different levels.

Religious and civic commemorations are also good opportunities for *mestres* to appear publicly. Such commemorations include the Lavagem do Bonfim in January,[7] the festivity of Iemanjá on 2 February in Rio Vermelho,[8] the celebration of Bahia's independence on 2 July, and New Year's Eve. These are considered special events for capoeira practitioners. At these occasions, as in workshops and the handing over of a title, the unity of the CAC is more visible.

Two dates deserve special attention for capoeira participants: 5 April and 21 November. The fifth of April is the birth date of the legendary Mestre Pastinha. It is perhaps the most important occasion: groups in Bahia and all over the world celebrate a commemoration of the so-called father of capoeira Angola. The ABCA holds a *roda* in Pelourinho, where the heirs of Mestre Pastinha come to pay their respect to the founding leader. In other academies there are talks and *rodas* that highlight the importance of Pastinha in the development of capoeira Angola. Many leaders use this date to give long speeches and old students of Pastinha are often invited to speak about his legacy. For many *mestres,* this day is the most important unifying moment in the CAC. By celebrating Pastinha's birthday, *mestres* also reflect on their roles as leaders and followers of this distinctive common tradition.

The twentieth of November is the Dia da Consciência Negra (Black Awareness Day) in Brazil, and commemorates the abolition of slavery (although the abolition date is officially celebrated on 13 May). In recent decades it has become an occasion to celebrate and praise all aspects of the Afro-Brazilian heritage in Brazil.

For many of Bahia's inhabitants, 20 November is a day to demand racial equity and respect, and a day to celebrate also the Afro-Brazilian hero Zumbi dos Palmares, a runaway slave whose local story reverberates in the collective imagination of the people as a symbol of freedom and emancipation. After escaping from slavery, Zumbi founded his own Quilombo (autonomous community of maroons) in Palmares. *Mestres* consider Zumbi to be an epic hero who fought against the Portuguese in the seventeenth century and who died tragically defending his Quilombo. For capoeira Angola practitioners, it is a day to show passionately their African roots. The figure of Zumbi is revered in the Angola community, and he is viewed as the forefather of capoeira. In fact, many *mestres* are convinced that Zumbi knew the martial art when he fought in the Quilombo dos Palmares. Many capoeira practitioners take part in this day by organizing *rodas* in the streets and taking part in demonstrations together with other important dance, music, and Candomblé groups.

The Members of the Academies

Mestres do not interact alone, and students are an important part in the constitution of social relations in the CAC. Students are classified according to six categories related to their hierarchical position in their academies: *contramestres, treinels,* professors, advanced students, regular students, beginners, and tourists.

An academy of capoeira Angola is formed of ten to twenty members and is enhanced by the presence of foreign practitioners who visit the academies year-round. In some cases, the number of foreigners exceeds that of local members, as often happened in the FICA. In general, locals form the group's core, although they may come from different backgrounds and different areas of the city. Academies are open to everybody, regardless of sex, race, and economic background. Students tend to belong to the middle class, however. Their average age is between sixteen and thirty years old. Some of them are students working toward a high school diploma or in the course of their university studies, and some have stable jobs. There is not a predominant presence of Afro-Brazilian students over white or others, although many groups such as ACANNE or GCAP work hard to encourage the participation and inclusion of black students in their classes. Although the practice has been opened to women in the past twenty-five years, there is still a slight discrimination against homosexuality in the groups, and only a few academies tolerate openly gay students.

Every capoeira academy charges an average of 50 Reais (approximately $15.54 in 2016) per month to its local members. Students with a difficult economic situation usually are not required to pay, and they can compensate the *mestre* in other ways for the lessons they take. For instance, they can help a *mestre* to clean the academy, fabricate musical instruments, and give occasional lessons for beginners.

An academy is organized under the strict supervision of the *mestre* who is in charge of the lessons, the logistics, and the finances of the group. Classes are held two or three times a week and *rodas* happen on the weekends. Many academies have been active for more than twenty years, and many *mestres* have graduated other *mestres* or *contramestres*. The overall number of members has changed throughout the years. In fact, the fluctuation and constancy of students is unstable; only a few students continue to practice longer than four or five years. They are likely to receive a title or take responsibility of the group while the *mestre* is away. The GCAP and the CECA, for example, are groups that have a constant presence of at least one or two *contramestres* and advanced students, accompanied by a fluctuating, irregular number of beginners and short-term students.

Students may switch groups, too. They may train intermittently, when they have the time. In this sense, their commitment is reduced to appearing at events or attending classes sporadically. *Contramestres*, professors, and *treinels* will leave their home groups at some point to open their own academies in other cities in Brazil or abroad. They carry the responsibility of their mentors, and they must be able to handle the command of a new group. In fact, the destiny of almost all the *treinels* and *contramestres*, I dare say, is to move out of their original groups in order to continue the work of their mentors.

Because the organization of an academy depends on the *mestre's* being in a position of power, dependency on his authority may bring troubles to his own project. For instance, he may face problems leading his group because of age or illness. His departure to another country could also undermine the organization of his academy, and could slowly create a decline of his power in it, resulting in internal struggles for the control of the empty place left by him.

In many cases, the death of a *mestre* means the end of his academy. Due to the constant mobility of members, sometimes the delegation of power from *mestre* to *contramestre* or to *treinel* does not occur. A *mestre* can lead his academy for twenty years and, at the end of his life, have only a few students left around him. He might also have nobody, like Mestre Pastinha. So power is not transferred to the experienced persons whom he has graduated, because his more advanced students are likely to have left the group a long time ago. They have their own academies and cannot take control of their old school. Struggles for power among the few remaining students can destroy the structure of a group, although the remaining students often form new groups.

Most *mestres* do not want to end their lives in abject poverty, as Mestre Pastinha did, so they focus on keeping their groups working as efficiently as possible. A successful mechanism for survival in recent years has been the transferring of authority to members of a *mestre's* family. In the past decade, *mestres* have trained their close relatives, mainly sons and nephews, in their academies, with the intention that these heirs will continue the work of their parents.

Final Remarks

The sociology of capoeira Angola presented in this chapter shows the diversity of relations created by the *mestres* and how they act as charismatic figures who hold a certain kind of power. I have focused on the contextual effects that such power engenders and the extent of its influence. The existence of a community of practitioners, lineages, and forms of adscriptions constitute a world in itself. It is within this contextual framework of relations that the actions of capoeira practitioners become meaningful. However, this does not mean that the sociology of capoeira supersedes or explains practice. My view is that the sociological context here presented has a recursive and dialectical relationship with the performative bodily acts of practitioners and with the cosmological contextual principles that guide them. So far, I have only described the contextual relations from a general perspective, but nothing has been said about practice and cosmology. Therefore, the next two chapters will focus on the latter two themes in order to give an account of the pragmatic force of capoeira Angola and its implications for the development of an anthropology of cosmological praxis.

Notes

1. The terms "professor" and "*treinel*" are of recent introduction. They were created by capoeira Angola *mestres* in order to offer a level of recognition to advanced students. These intermediate titles allow a more stable control of the persons who are in line to become *contramestres*.
2. Salvador's historic center is divided in lower and upper "cities". The upper city is located on the top of a hill while the lower city runs along the coast. This division in upper and lower cities is similar to the one found in Lisbon, Portugal.
3. For an excellent study about the impact of tourism in the practice of capoeira in Salvador, see Hedegard (2013).
4. This is an initiative that has its origins in a project designed in 1997 to renew the Forte Santo Antônio Além do Carmo, a building that at the time was rapidly deteriorating. Although facing constant financial and bureaucratic difficulties, in 2005 the renewal project took place. The justification to do it was to create a center for the diffusion and preservation of capoeira. The renovation was finally concluded at the end of 2006. Today, three of the most important capoeira academies have their headquarters there.
5. For a more detailed discussion about the different marketing strategies employed by capoeira practitioners, see Almeida et al. (2013).
6. Viva meu mestre.. quem me ensinou a capoeira!
7. This celebration takes part over the whole of Salvador's lower city on 12 January. It runs from the church of the Conceição da Praia to the Bonfim church. In this celebration, many capoeira *rodas* are held in the streets. During my time in Salvador, I counted three street *rodas* organized by Regional groups and one organized by the ABCA at the main stairs of the Bonfim church.
8. On this day, a multitude of persons devoted to the Afro-Brazilian religion of Candomblé congregate close to the ritual precinct dedicated to the goddess of water, a mermaid who gives protection to sailors. Many Capoeira players and *mestres* attend this festivity to pay respect and reverence to Iemanjá, who is the patroness of many Angola academies. (I have not yet discovered why she is revered and no other Candomblé gods are.) In recent years it has become popular to hold *rodas* commemorating Iemanjá. The most well-known gathering is in the academy of Grupo Nzinga. The Angola players do not perform in the streets on this day, although capoeira players belonging to other styles do. During my time in the festivity, I registered three *rodas* organized in the streets by Regional groups, and they were open to the public. In the Nzinga academy things looked more private and closed. Although it was a free event and open to everybody, the participants in attendance were members from the Angola community, including six *mestres* and a large number of students from seven different groups. The *roda* lasted around three hours and was complemented with Samba, *feijoada* (a classic dish made of beans), and beers.

CHAPTER 3

℔ Cosmological Bodies

The history and sociology of capoeira Angola in Bahia presented in chapters 1 and 2 set up the social context of a ritual practice. Practice cannot be detached from the general framework in which it is deployed, so my effort so far has been to offer an overview of the histories and relations that emerge from the interactions of humans within a ritual, performative practice. My objective in this chapter is to shift the focus of the description of capoeira Angola from a historical and sociological perspective to a detailed ethnographic account of bodily practice and its cosmological foundations. Therefore, this chapter deals specifically with the different connotations of the notion of the *corpo fechado* in capoeira Angola, because it is an intrinsic element for understanding embodiment, cosmology, and symbolism in the practice. I delve into analysis of the bodily dimension of capoeira in order to clarify the recursive relationship between the particularity of performance and the general context described in the previous chapter.

The practice of capoeira Angola refers to bodies in movement and to symbolic interpretations of those bodies. I analyze the body from a theoretical standpoint that acknowledges the importance of a phenomenological perspective and semiotics, although I attempt to build a more general argument that links these two approaches with the issue of cosmology.

The relevance of phenomenological and semiotic perspectives in the study of capoeira are outlined in two of the most important anthropological works available in the English language about the Afro-Brazilian art (Downey 2005; Lewis 1992, 1995), and recently in a philosophical/ Piercian analysis that reflects on the relationship between capoeira and Afro-Brazilian religions (Merrel 2005). While I agree that phenomenology and semiotics address different analytical levels of capoeira, they do not unify these levels. The relationship between the body and the cultural context where practice occurs seems fragmented, inconsistent, and almost broken in these approaches. On the one hand, phenomenological anthropology has focused on the role that experience and embodiment play in culture, as exemplified, for instance, by the works of Thomas Csordas (1990) and Michael Jackson (1983). However, in their attempt to extricate the intimate process of experience, these researchers have taken for granted the political and cosmological contexts where embodiment is performed. In the work of Greg Downey, which builds on the work of Jackson and the inspirational work of Loïc Wacquant (2006) on boxing, the richness of his phenomenological description of capoeira ignores the contextual sociopolitical relations in which this art form is immersed and his description does not extensively address the issues of power and cosmology.

On the other hand, the metaphor of "culture as a text" that is found at the core of French semiotics (made famous by Clifford Geertz [2000]) does not give enough credit to the role of the individual in the process of interpretation and meaningful creation. Although I am not suggesting the glorification of the individual as the path to follow in anthropology in any case, in capoeira one cannot dismiss the role of charismatic persons as symbols of cosmological power. The work of Lowell Lewis provides a wonderful description of the most important textual elements of capoeira in Bahia, but does not effectively relate this discursive aspect with bodily action. Instead, the work presents the discursive and the body as unconnected domains.

From my point of view, semiotics and cultural phenomenology complement each other. They form part of a relational context of mutual implication—what Roy Wagner has described as a recursive effect (Wagner 1986a, 2001) and other anthropologists have defined as the implication of part and whole in a holistic view of culture (Ingold 2005: 45–80; Mosko 2010; Strathern 1995). Therefore, I consider symbolic interpretation, action, and bodily experience to form a unified whole in capoeira Angola. In this chapter, therefore, I intend to show how this unity is displayed by addressing the importance of the concept of the *corpo fechado* in the levels of bodily, cosmological, and symbolic interaction.

The *corpo fechado* is a recurrent concept among capoeira practitioners, particularly *mestres*. It refers both to bodily actions in the *rodas* and to symbolic, spiritual, and cosmological forces. Therefore, this concept condenses different connotations to evoke what Philippe Descola (1988, 2005) has defined as a relation between cosmology and practice, which stands in a recursive relation between the forces of cosmological principles and the performance of bodily actions.

The logic of practice refers intimately to the physical dimension of the *corpo fechado*, particularly as concerns how participants learn about and understand the concept. It also contains symbolic connotations that go beyond the realm of embodiment and that evoke magic, spiritual, and religious elements of Afro-Brazilian culture. There is the issue of cosmology. The *corpo fechado*, in a more abstract sense, establishes a set of basic principles that capoeira Angola shares with the religion of Candomblé. By considering these two practices to pertain to a common cosmology, one may conceive of the *corpo fechado* as a form of cosmo-praxis. This does not mean that all capoeira practitioners or *mestres* have to subscribe to the religion of Candomblé, however. The cosmological matrix shared by both Afro-Brazilian practices highlight the profound link between them, but that does not indicate that capoeira *mestres* must belong to Candomblé houses. In fact, many Catholic or evangelical capoeira leaders consider the closeness between capoeira and Candomblé as pernicious and strongly condemn any reference between the practice and the Afro-Brazilian religion.

The Logic of Practice: Learning about the *Corpo Fechado*

The logic of capoeira Angola is based on a face-to-face interaction between two persons (also called practitioners or players) in close contact in a reduced space. This space is the *roda*, which is the circle in which capoeira is played (see Figure 3.1). Its dimensions may vary, but each *roda* has a diameter between 4.80 and 7.32 meters wide.

The objective of capoeira is not to attack directly an opponent. On the contrary, the aim is to mislead the other person through use of cunning, astute, and deceptive movements, which Brazilians define generally as *malícia*. Cunning and deception are seen as strategies to open the adversary's body, which will show his vulnerabilities. The logic of practice indicates that the interaction is basically a *jogo* (game) of questions and answers. For example, to any feigned attack corresponds a similar and reciprocal counterattack. Attacks are performed by kicks, *rasteiras* (leg-sweeps), *cabeçadas* (head-butts), and occasionally the use of grabbing techniques. Defensive movements do not block the attacks but evade them. In order to play well, one needs to escape, avoid contact, and flow with the game.

As Greg Downey (2005: 160–67) has shown, the process of learning capoeira means perceiving many things at the same time and devel-

Figure 3.1. The *roda* of Capoeira Angola at Associação de Capoeira Angola Navio Negreiro (ACANNE). Photograph: Sergio González Varela. Date: 18 March 2006.

oping a sideways glance. For instance, an advanced student or a *mestre* can develop a peripheral vision in order to see hidden intentions. Downey considers learning how to use this oblique perception to be a perceptual scheme exclusive to capoeira Angola. It is a process of experiential knowledge that readjusts the practitioner's experience of being in the world.

The *corpo fechado* in this level of ethnographic description refers to specific parts of the body. According to my informants, the body parts considered vulnerable to attack are the face, thorax, and legs. All the informants perceived the face to be the most vulnerable part, as a kick or a *cabeçada* in the nose or mouth can cause a great deal of damage. The thorax attracted the attention of the *mestres* and was their greatest object of scrutiny; during lessons, they often indicated to students that exposure of the thorax was dangerous and a symptom of vulnerability and weakness for any practitioner, particularly when executing acrobatic or defensive moves (see illustration 3.2). Legs needed to be protected because they could be caught in a leg-sweep, making a capoeira player lose his balance. Giving the back to one's opponent was also considered dangerous, and *mestres* always emphasized that a practitioner should always keep his eyes on his adversary. However, turning one's back to an opponent is a way to avoid being hit in the face by a *cabeçada*.

In principle, there are no prescriptions about what body parts practitioners shall or shall not hit, but I often witnessed situations in which *mestres* were upset about certain kinds of kicks. For instance, they deplored the idea of kicking to the knees or genitals of an opponent; they also considered a slap of a player's buttocks of a player, the throwing of punches, and the execution of leg-sweeps to a practitioner who was in a handstand to be disrespectful maneuvers.

To achieve a *corpo fechado* is very difficult, and requires a long process of learning and practice. In the case of beginners, recognition develops through mastering and controlling the body and by being aware of the vulnerable positions above described. For advanced students, one of the keys is to learn how to combine gracious bodily movements that can deceive an opponent to open his body while at the same time protecting your own.

Figure 3.2. Mestre Boca do Rio closing his body while doing a headstand. Photograph: Sergio González Varela. Date: 18 August 2006.

Recognizing vulnerable body parts is essential to gaining an understanding of capoeira because it evinces capoeira's potential to be a dangerous practice. As I have mentioned previously, practitioners aim to achieve a knowledge of how to use cunning and avoid physical violence. This means that the strategy used to open a body must include misleading and deceptive acts, preferably acrobatic and skillful moves.

Although there are plenty of deceptive physical movements and attitudes in capoeira Angola, the repertoire of kicks available is fairly limited compared to those available in other capoeira styles and martial arts. During my research, I registered six basic kicks: *meia lua de frente* (front half-moon kick), *rabo de arraia* (stingray's tail kick), *martelo* (hammer), *armada* (a stingray kick without hands), *meia lua de costas* (back half-moon kick), and *benção* (blessing kick); two basic defensive moves: *negativa* (negation) and *role* (a low turn using the hands); and four counter-attacks: *cabeçada* (head-butt), *tesoura* (scissor kick), *chapa* (plate kick), and *rasteira* (leg-sweep).

While this list seems rather schematic, the use of body techniques becomes more complicated when we realize that what counts is not how many attacking or defensive movements exist or that a player can execute. What matters is how a player can use these moves creatively to deceive an opponent or to escape from an exposed situation. One of the most amazing capoeira Angola bodily interactions occur when two players don't fall into the trap of deception and can escape and attack fluidly in a way that combines a whole set of acrobatic movements.

During lessons, a *mestre* pays particular attention to the exposed situations of openness that students display in practice, which he tries to correct and later use to explore possible counterattacks or escapes. *Mestres* emphasize that the awareness of vulnerable positions during training is a vital element in the development of a proper game strategy. When students have grasped and assimilated the most intrinsic aspects of the game, they have to gain experience by participating and playing with more-experienced players in the *rodas*. This provides them the opportunity to practice what they have learned in the classroom.

Capoeira Angola practitioners must attend to the degree of openness and exposure that their movements reveal. For instance, an open *aú* (cartwheel) may leave the thorax vulnerable to a *cabeçada;* a front kick may be susceptible to a *rasteira* if one is not careful. Accordingly, to attack with a *cabeçada* without protecting the face may prompt an adversary to push with his knee as a defense, hitting directly the nose and mouth of the individual executing the *cabeçada*.

In the *roda,* deception and simulation are paramount, and there is more to these two concepts than ways of using the body. Behind the concepts lies hidden a whole set of connotations of power that I will describe in detail in the next chapter. For the moment, I would like to mention that the development of deceptive skills begins with the process of learning about the *corpo fechado.* This is the first level of embodied practice, and it is the most important capoeira attitude to acquire and master.

Capoeira Angola practitioners consider a *mestre* to be a master of deception. He can mislead an adversary and surprise him with unexpected attacks. He can wrap his real intentions with beautiful acrobatic movements in order to seduce and defeat an opponent. He can laugh and seem amicable and relaxed. However, he is preparing to betray his opponent. He is using deception in order to attack and open a body. On the surface, it is not possible to guess the real intentions of *mestres* in capoeira, because they have mastered the art of remaining closed and their intentions are protected.

As part of the process of learning capoeira Angola, a practitioner needs to learn how to execute *chamadas* (calls). A *chamada* is a movement used to stop the flow of the game (Lewis 1992: 120). A player stands in the middle of the *roda* with open arms or gives his back and invites the adversary to come closer (see Figure 3.3). The adversary ac-

Figure 3.3. Mestre Boca do Rio performing a *chamada.* Photograph: Sergio González Varela. Date: 8 August 2016.

cepts the *chamada* and both players walk to and fro holding hands or embracing. The *chamada* ends when the player who started it invites his adversary to resume the game.

According to Mestre Boca do Rio, a *chamada* is as dangerous as any other capoeira move because a player remains exposed during a brief period. Boca said that practitioners know how to perform four basic *chamadas: chamada de frente* (front *chamada*), *chamada de Cristo de frente* (front Christ *chamada*), *chamada de Cristo de costas* (back Christ *chamada*), and *sapinho* (little toad). Lowell Lewis (1992) has defined the *chamadas* as a game within the game, and he identifies a sequenced structure of six steps for each *chamada* that are generally followed by practitioners (Lewis 1992: 121):

1. Call
2. Response
3. The approach
4. The waltz
5. The separation
6. Resume normal play

The reasons to perform a *chamada* vary. The following four specific situations might cause a *chamada*: (1) When the player realizes that something is going wrong in the *roda*. (2) When the exposure of one's vulnerable bodily parts occurs. (3) When a practitioner opens the body of an adversary. (4) When a practitioner wants to challenge an adversary. In the first case, a practitioner may do a *chamada* if the music is not being played correctly, or if a song is not apt for the moment. In the second and third cases, a *chamada* is executed after a player has hit an adversary or has been caught by a *rasteira* or a *cabeçada*. In the latter case, a *chamada* may indicate the beginning of a challenge between two players. It is important to mention that when a challenge occurs a simple game could transform into a fight with unexpected consequences, particularly when the two opponents are famous and powerful *mestres*.

Narratives about the *Corpo Fechado*

Away from the *roda*, references to the *corpo fechado* evoke narratives related to the old *mestres* and their violent past (Dias 2006). During my research, I was engaged in conversations with *mestres* who eagerly recalled their deeds when they were young, amazing stories about dangerous *rodas* in which they took part, narratives that were filled up with nostalgia about the times when playing capoeira Angola was a serious and dangerous matter rather than something for tourists. The *mestres* also talked profusely about their own *mestres*. For instance, one leader remembered how his *mestre* met his most acerbic enemy during a trip abroad, and they had to play one another with no chance to escape or avoid the interaction; the game ended cordially, but it was very tense and strenuous, because the *mestres* hated each other.

Other times *mestres* recalled their best *rasterias* and their best movements against other famous *mestres*. Kenneth Dossar (1992: 8) mentioned that most of the narrative of capoeira Angola has to do with keeping an epic mythology alive, through which practitioners connect to their past and the dead. It is in this conversational context that comments about the *corpo fechado* form part of the epic history of the *mestres*.

Expressions found about the *corpo fechado* during an interaction in a *roda* vary depending on the Angola academy one is visiting. Among the most recurrent were *cair pra dentro do jogador* (go inside, and put pressure on a player), *apertar o jogo* (push the game), *cobrar do adversário* (pay back or test an adversary). These expressions have the objective of giving warnings to players about situations of openness, describing how to play and interact in the *roda*.

Other comments about the *corpo fechado* appear in songs that evoke the importance of protection. For instance, when a player falls down or has been shown a leg-sweep, the audience may react by emitting a hushed exhalation. Consequently, the lead singer changes to a song with the following lyrics:

> My machete struck down
> The banana tree fell down
> Fall, fall banana tree
> The banana tree fell down.[1]

Music provides a commentary to the audience about the development of a game. For the most part, experienced practitioners take the responsibility of leading the music and taking control of the *rodas*. Therefore, when a player succeeds in opening and getting through another player's body, this is either praised in song or addressed in mockery against the vulnerability of the opened person.

There are no songs that use specifically the words "*corpo fechado*"; the majority of references appear as animal metaphors. For instance, they might describe a dangerous player—someone who can easily open others' bodies—as a snake, such as in this song:

> That snake bites me
> Saint Benedict
> She is venomous
> Saint Benedict.[2]

So far I have described those elements that form part of the logic of practice in capoeira Angola and how they relate to the protection and vulnerability of the body. The concept of the *corpo fechado,* however, goes beyond the realm of bodily practice. There is another level, at which the *corpo fechado* takes on a new meaning. The symbolic domain has often been obviated in phenomenological anthropology, where the logic of practice relates fundamentally to a set of spiritual connotations. Beyond the level of embodiment lies an ambit where the *corpo fechado* establishes a cosmological set of principles that are shared with the Afro-Brazilian religion of Candomblé.

Symbolic and Spiritual Connotations of the *Corpo Fechado*: The Relationship between Capoeira Angola and Candomblé

The bodily techniques of the *corpo fechado* described in the previous section form the foundation for a set of symbolic connotations. These connotations transcend the materiality of the body. The process of learning about techniques and strategies is just a first step toward understanding capoeira Angola holistically. There has always been a deeper meaning behind capoeira's logic of practice.

Merleau-Ponty famously said that being in the world condemns one to finding meaning (Merleau-Ponty 2005: xxii). The act of recognizing and embodying an understanding of the *corpo fechado* is to gain control of a meaningful perception; it is a preobjective apprehension of cultural knowledge. The apprehension that emerges from the body but transcends it is what I call the symbolic.

If we are condemned to experiencing meaning, then there is a relation of complementarity between embodiment and symbolism that must be addressed. In my experience among capoeira Angola groups, this complementarity draws attention to the importance of a set of immaterial procedures that provide the *corpo fechado* with an enhanced potential to defeat adversaries. Although the distinction between material and immaterial is never clear-cut in capoeira Angola, the *corpo fechado* is the connector between practice and the invisible substance of power considered secret or ineffable by *mestres*. More about the implications of this invisibility will be shown in the next chapter. For now, this discussion will show how the *corpo fechado* transcends practice and embodiment.

I consider the distinction between material and immaterial to be mainly analytical. The distinction is deployed here in order to clarify an anthropological argumentative description of inseparable categories in practice during the *rodas*. The *corpo fechado* is a totality; what we see in a *roda* is the product of an endless work of practitioners behind the scenes, of physical moves trained daily in the classroom, and of individuals prepared spiritually to achieve closure. The immaterial is thus made evident in practice, and it is indistinguishable from it. Practice and symbolism become one in the bodies of those who are the experts in closing their bodies: the *mestres*. This oneness is at the core of my definition of embodiment.

Before delving into the consequences of uniting a symbol with its reference, however, I would like to describe the core of the symbolic aspects of capoeira Angola.

According to the *mestres* I worked with, capoeira Angola cannot be dissociated from an African religious and ideological context.[3] They told me that, with few exceptions, most capoeira Angola *mestres* in Bahia were related to the religion of Candomblé in some way or another. They said that it was possible to affirm that Candomblé was their religion. Simone Ponde Vassallo mentions that capoeira practitioners have turned to Candomblé as a form of finding and justifying a true African spiritual connection, and Candomblé is the closest they can find (Vassallo 2005: 179). I agree with Vassallo, and I would just add that, even though some *mestres* do not want to be involved in Candomblé nowadays because they are Christians or belong to other religions, they still preserve in capoeira many cosmological aspects that refer to an Afro-Brazilian religious tradition.

There is not room or scope in this book to discuss in detail the anthropology of Candomblé, so I will give a general description of this Afro-Brazilian religion by stressing its most important elements. There are three types of Candomblé denominated by nations: Jejé, Angola, and Ketu. The differences among nations are distinctive elements like clothes, dance, music, ritual, liturgy, linguistic origins, and historical backgrounds (Bastide 1978: 194). For instance, the Jejé nation is associated linguistically and historically with Benin's Fon tradition, the Ketu nation with the Yoruba tradition of Nigeria, and the Angola nation with the Bantu tradition of Congo and Angola.

Although there are many differences between the three types of Candomblé, all share a set of divinities called *orixás* that manifest during rituals in ceremonial houses called *terreiros* (shrine). The number of *orixás* may vary depending on the characteristics of every nation, but according to Roger Bastide (1978: 195) there are between thirteen to sixteen *orixás* within the general cosmological pantheon of Candomblé. Marcio Goldman (2005: 103) mentions that all variants of Candomblé are based on initiation ceremonies; in all, learning how to interact with the *orixás* takes a lifetime. Some include animal sacrifices, while some do not.

Mestres and advanced students of capoeira Angola (mainly those who are involved in the organization of the academies) are active members of Candomblé *terreiros*. Some *mestres* even hold honorary titles in the *terreiros*, due to their acknowledged role as Afro-Brazilian ambassadors. Younger *mestres* are initiated in the formal hierarchy of Candomblé; they could be *filhos de santo* (sons of saint, which is the initial stage), *ogans* (those responsible for the ritual music), or simply devotees. Because of their busy agendas, *mestres* cannot be committed full time to their *terreiros*. Nevertheless, they try to stay connected with their religion as much as their time allows.

Within Candomblé's religious hierarchy, the *pais de santo* (father of saint) and the *mães de santo* (mothers of saint) are the spiritual leaders of the ceremonial houses. They are the closest persons in contact with the *orixás* (Wafer 1991). They are also the moral guides of the *mestres*. Leaders of capoeira keep their relationship with their *pais* and *mães de santo* in strictly personal terms. By this I mean they do not talk often in their academies about their spiritual leaders or their religious views. Initially, they stress that a student does not need to be involved in Candomblé or any particular religion at all to practice capoeira. Although this is in part true, in a more personal level some of my friends admitted that becoming an apprentice of Candomblé is a fundamental step for a student if he or she wants to ascend in the CAC's hierarchy of power. In fact, some of the *mestres* I worked with learned about Candomblé through capoeira and not the other way around.

Rituals of Protection and Secrecy

Modern capoeira Angola in Bahia is heavily influenced by Candomblé. This has had repercussions on the symbolic connotation of the *corpo fechado* in practice. According to Mestre Cobra Mansa, to achieve a *corpo fechado* or to make sense of all its implications takes many years, decades, a whole life dedicated to capoeira. It has to do with practice, but also with an understanding of other elements of Afro-Brazilian culture. In this sense, to close the body becomes a holistic practice. It is something that a *mestre* must understand not only when he is training capoeira or in the *rodas,* but also in the activities of his daily life. It is a form of life that demands from a *mestre* a constant awareness of any potential dangers in life that may leave his body unprotected. This affects his perception, attitudes, and interpersonal relations.

Leaders do not like to interact with one another or play together in the *rodas.* If they do, the game is normally a very careful and polite encounter. After learning about the *corpo fechado,* one attains another understanding of the politics of capoeira Angola. Through a life dedicated to learning an embodied practice, *mestres* create a form of habitus that directs and builds their social and interpersonal relations.

To close the body is to remain symbolically distant and protected, to avoid situations of possible danger and risk. This closure is exemplified by *mestres'* attitude of mistrust toward others. Their mistrust implies that they must be careful with the kinds of interpersonal relations in which they engage. Mistrust may also help explain the annoyance that many students feel when, after years of training, they still have not been able to gain the trust of their mentors. The dictates of the *corpo fechado* may never allow such a degree of confidence. In fact, *mestres* often said to me that they expect that an act of treason will be executed either by the leader or the student in the capoeira academy as part of the process of learning about capoeira and as a lesson about life in general. In the *rodas,* songs about treason abound, along with stories where students betray their *mestres* or where *mestres* are let down by those they trusted.

The notion of betrayal makes protection a necessary strategy of survival. With the idea of treason in mind, *mestres* become even more careful in their acts and in their focus on the symbolic connotations of the *corpo fechado.* There are many ways a body can be closed symbolically. The most common one is to ask the religious authorities of

Candomblé for protection before a *roda* or workshop. This symbolic protection also extends to all those who enter the academies, because this space is considered an extension of the body of the *mestres*. I witnessed *mestres* treating their academies like shrines, with small altars placed in key positions to provide protection. The walls were also painted with motifs depicting three or more *orixás*. Before a *roda*, *mestres* lead a symbolic cleansing of the bad energies that may have existed around the academies.

A second way to close the body symbolically includes personal rituals of purification. Although these personal rituals are not followed by all *mestres* of capoeira Angola, they include general notions about cleanness and purification before a *roda*. The practitioners' bodies need to be immaculate; *mestres* bathe with a special concoction of herbs and they take care not to ingest too much alcohol the previous night. They also be sure to avoid sexual relations before a *roda*, because, as in many other ritual practices worldwide, sexual acts are considered to weaken the body, leaving it unprotected and vulnerable to attack. *Mestres* also believe that sexual abstinence stimulates the faculties of perception, enhances their physical energy, and helps to close their bodies more rapidly. Although sexual abstinence is something desirable, *mestres* do not follow the prohibition strictly. I have seen *mestres* negotiating the proscription and exchanging it with another kind of abstention, like fasting or not drinking alcohol.

One of the most important ritual procedures to close the body is the use of material objects like rings, necklaces, bracelets, coins, and stones. Of these amulets, the most important are *patuás* (necklaces made of plastic beads). A *patuá* is a visual reference of belonging to certain *orixás*. In fact, at least for *mestres* of capoeira Angola, *patuás* contain the *orixás*. That is why *patuás* are essential items for capoeira and Candomblé practitioners, because they signify a particular relationship between persons and *terreiros* and remit to an Afro-Brazilian identity. These necklaces are of extreme value because they bring a spiritual protection to practitioners; they are sacred objects. The use of *patuás* reminds me of Marcel Mauss's remarks related to the magic and power of objects: "We do find very clearly in magic the idea of objects possessing infinite powers: salt, blood, saliva, coral, iron, crystals, precious metals, the mountain ash, the birch, the sacred fig, camphor, incense, tobacco, etc., all incorporate general magical forces susceptible of application or specific use" (Mauss 2005: 127).

While capoeira Angola *mestres* use *patuás* and other amulets for protection, protection becomes another way of referring to the *corpo fechado*. *Patuás* protect because they close the body of the practitioners against vulnerabilities in the *rodas*. It is as if the *orixás* are at work invisibly any time *mestres* play capoeira, which is why they adopt such extreme carefulness anytime they interact with one another. A game between *mestres* is, in essence, a clash of powers.

Patuás can be worn visibly as necklaces or they may remain hidden from view in trouser pockets. In some cases, when a *mestre* wants to show he is "clean" and does not need any "extra" protection, he may remove his *patuás* and put them on the floor. Although it is not a common feat, I have seen *mestres* come clean of their *patuás* when they want to show their bare power, or when they feel they have nothing special to hide.

Despite the protection offered by amulets, a *mestre* is always at risk of being exposed when facing a more powerful opponent. There is a possibility of losing one's strength or capacity of closing the body if another practitioner is more intelligent and astute. In this case, a *chamada* may become more than a game within the game; it can transform into a power struggle for control. In this sense, a *chamada* is performed as an open challenge against closed bodies. To accept or reject a *chamada* in a *roda* becomes a serious business for a practitioner, because status and prestige are at stake.

The perception of the *corpo fechado* by *mestres* therefore involves knowledge not only of bodily techniques but also of personal rituals related to the spiritual and religious influence of Candomblé. Of course, not all *mestres* are practitioners of this Afro-Brazilian religion and, in those cases, the spirituality of capoeira is influenced by other religions like Catholicism, evangelism, or Pentecostalism.

The two levels of the *corpo fechado* should not be seen as two different domains that divide the material from the immaterial. In practice, both the symbolic and the embodied *corpo fechado* become one. It is during the stance of interaction in a *roda* that the symbolic gains its effectiveness by bringing spiritual protection and support. Learning about the *corpo fechado* is, above all, a holistic, integral process of knowledge—and an endless process, as *mestres* often mention. They believe that the knowledge of capoeira in general cannot be grasped completely in a lifetime. The meaning of the *corpo fechado* expands gradually as a practitioner advances in his life. The more time a practitioner spends learning about capoeira with a *mestre,* the more he will understand the magnitude of such knowledge. Obviously, to get to know the effects of the *corpo fechado* in the long term implies a strategy that can span many years or even decades, as in Candomblé.

The *Corpo Fechado* as Cosmo-Praxis

The concept of the *corpo fechado* in its experiential and symbolic levels is also linked to another important concept that will be discussed in the next chapter, called *mandinga. Mandinga* refers to the inner secret power of capoeira that holds a body closed and impenetrable. The body needs protection in order to accumulate power. The expressive evidence of a powerful *corpo fechado* involves supernatural feats like animal identification, prediction, and anticipation of movements, as well as longevity. A *corpo fechado* is the filter through which power is channeled and made visible.

In a more abstract sense, the *corpo fechado* refers to cosmological principles. According to Don Handelman (2008: 181), cosmological principles form the constitution of universals. When one is using the concept of cosmology, therefore, one is implicitly referring to ontological claims about being. In this way, cosmology sets up relations, divisions, and connections between principles and cultural expressions (Handelman 2008: 182). I agree with Handelman: his approach leads to an improved understanding of the cosmological dimension of the *corpo fechado.*

In capoeira Angola there is a cosmological principle that rejects a separation between the material and the immaterial, or between practice and symbolism. The division between the visible and the invisible, which echoes the familiar Western distinction between mind and body, does not appear to be effective for an understanding of capoeira. The inner logic of embodiment contains already the inseparability between symbols and references (the latter being the bodies of the practitioners). The symbolic means of protection are fused with the knowledge of practice. The analytical distinction used discursively in this chapter should be seen as a strategy to describe the different meanings of the *corpo fechado* and not as a condition of being. What we have is a recursive movement between perspectives. Humans and nonhumans interact closely, so protection against negative forces is paramount for practitioners and ritual action makes evident the dangers of the game.

Here, we are not dealing merely with representations, but also with presentations (see Holbraad 2008a) of the *corpo fechado* that effectively show who has knowledge and power and who has not.

To say that the experience of the *corpo fechado* could be explained just in the domain of beliefs, where practitioners believe that they are executing magical acts as a result of their protected bodies or amulets, is to undermine the inclusive and recursive effects between cosmology and practice. Handelman (2008: 188) noted that the uses of belief as a recourse for explaining non-Western cosmological principles is often a consequence of a monotheist, cosmic logic that consigns paradoxical or alien conceptions to the realm of the implausible. Belief in this context of explaining alterity could lead us to an ethnocentric perspective where other people in other cultures hold false or misguided perspectives about the world.

The cosmological implications of the *corpo fechado* form part of a more general and inclusive perception of Afro-Brazilian culture that encompasses Candomblé and capoeira. There are continuities and flows between both practices, and these are related to material and spiritual procedures, specific cultural rules, a common ancestry, and a plural cosmology. By plural cosmology, I reference the existence of a proliferation of beings that do not refer necessarily to a radical separation between a unique *orixá* and humans. On the contrary, this cosmology allows for humans and nonhumans to coexist and interact in capoeira *rodas* and Candomblé ceremonies.

The cosmological continuity between Candomblé and capoeira Angola remits, initially, to what Floyd Merrel calls a non-Western alternative logic (Merrel 2005). Although I agree with Merrel concerning the cultural differentiation between Afro-Brazilian practices and other cultural forms, I cannot help associating his view with that of Lévy-Bruhl and his idea of a radical, prelogic, primitive mentality (Lévy-Bruhl 1923: 35–58). Lévy Bruhl presented the relationship between "primitives" and "moderns" as one based on a radical differentiation with no common ground between them; the alterity between them was insurmountable due to the "prelogical" status of the "primitives."

Nothing like this is suggested here by the allusion to a plural cosmology. I do not support the idea that Afro-Brazilians have such radically different cultures from others, as perhaps the reading of Merrel might suggest. However, the way in which the proliferation of beings appears in capoeira and Candomblé demands that we take such proliferation seriously. The cosmological principles of the *corpo fechado* imply ontological and epistemological disjunctions about what unites and moves the cosmos.

The cosmological continuity between capoeira and Candomblé also shows differences and particularities when relating to the multiplicity of beings that appear in both practices. These beings (human and nonhuman) emerge from the same pluralist organizational cosmological matrix, in my view. The existence of this organizational core validates statements that have been defined as Afrocentric by academics (Assunção 2005), such as the evocation of Africa in *mestres'* discourses and the fascination of people to searching the African origins of Brazilian life and culture. Again, the *mestres* assume themselves to be descendants of an African tradition introduced to Brazil through slavery. For many *mestres*, capoeira and Candomblé are the result of a common history of violence, exploitation, racism, and denigration of the black population. In this sense, both Afro-Brazilian practices are forms of cultural resistance and resilience. They form part of a historical continuity of oppression that goes back to the introduction of slavery to the North and South American continents.

Many *mestres* trace the origin of capoeira back to a ritual in Angola called N'golo (Cascudo 1967; GCAP and ACANNE 1989). Candomblé traces its origins to different African traditions, too. Although there is more evidence concerning the African origins of Candomblé in its similarities to African religions in Benin, Angola, and Nigeria (Matory 2005; Parés 2006), in the case of capoeira, neither academic nor nonacademic studies have found conclusive evidence of its African ritual origins (Cascudo 1967; Desch-Obi 2000).

Notwithstanding the difficulties of finding reliable evidence about the past, *mestres* would not consider capoeira Angola as just a Brazilian art form. In a cosmological sense, the notion of African continuity means also an unbroken temporal succession. Therefore, *mestres* assume that they belong to a past that they actualize every time they practice capoeira. From their point of view, to close their bodies is a way of reproducing the past; it establishes a crucial relationship with the dead and their African ancestors. The effects of temporal disjunction are some of the aspects that distinguish *mestres* from the rest of practitioners, because they do not consider themselves to share the same temporality with others. They deny coevalness, or the sense of belonging to the same contemporaneous time (Fabian 1983), when they relate to others.

Ethnographically what I found working with *mestres* of capoeira was that these individuals consider the denial of coevalness (Birth 2008) to be an act of power and a form to set up the hierarchical relations in the CAC; it was a mode of differentiation that complemented the knowledge gained through embodiment and learning symbolically about the *corpo fechado*. Social hierarchies also then represent temporal hierarchies.

Evidence of a Plural Cosmology

Temporal and cultural continuity are vital to building an understanding of the cosmology of capoeira Angola, and homologous to the kind of spiritual continuity one finds among Candomblé practitioners, where the intercrossing between divinities and humans is common. There are differences between capoeira and Candomblé, however, regarding their relations with nonhumans.

A plural cosmological expression of Candomblé is the proliferation of *orixás,* because these *orixás* have the ability to develop new relations, from which new *orixás* may find their way into the world. The manifestation of divinities through possession rituals is paramount. Possession is a way to get to know the *orixás* and their personalities.

In capoeira Angola, *mestres* say that there is a multiplicity of beings, among them the *orixás,* who may or may not manifest in the *roda*. However, they consider that allowing an *orixá* to take possession of them would be dangerous. *Orixás* protect practitioners by being contained in amulets, but they must be kept at bay. In this sense, Angelo Decanio has argued that it is impossible to engage in a trance in capoeira in the same fashion that possession occurs in Candomblé (Decanio 2001c: 43), due to the risk of losing control of the body. There is no chance for an *orixá* to take possession of a *mestre*. Decanio's position is that the mediation between humans and divinities never implies full spirit possession. He mentions that capoeira practitioners can interact with *orixás* and other beings without losing consciousness by entering what he refers to as "a situation of semi-trance" (Decanio 2001c: 43).

Apart from *orixás,* there are other spiritual beings surrounding the performances of capoeira Angola that help practitioners to keep their bodies closed and protected and that are not exclusively linked to Candomblé. The most important ones are the spirits of the dead *mestres* and the African ancestors. For instance, Mestre Boca do Rio often said that there are more spectators in the audience of a *roda* than one could perceive at first glance. He said that a *mestre* knows that there are spirits among the public, too. He said that a good *roda* attracts the attention of dead *mestres* who may decide to take part in it if they are feeling the energy and the music. The dead *mestres* contribute to the development of a *roda*. They can help a practitioner to defeat an adversary by providing an extra source of energy.

Although Boca did not explain where the dead *mestres* were located in the *roda*, he said that many *mestres* perform for the dead *mestres* or other beings; that for *mestres*, dead *mestres* are their main audience. Mestre Boca do Rio also mentioned that this was not a metaphor to embellish his narrative—it was something real. He told me, "The dead are real and you can feel their presence if you have the ability to perceive them and if you have the power to invoke them." Because there is a plurality of spiritual beings surrounding the practice of capoeira Angola, protection and keeping a *corpo fechado* are serious matters. There are many things at stake, and a *mestre* is aware of the dangers this implies.

The similarities between capoeira Angola and Candomblé extend to the perception of a plurality of beings and the deployment of a plurality of cosmological forces. In Candomblé these forces are the *orixás*, whereas in capoeira they include *orixás* as well as the spirits of the dead *mestres* and African ancestors. In both Afro-Brazilian practices we perceive a continuity of cultural formations and temporal connotations. Both practices belong to the same cosmological multiple principles. They are part of what Mestre Renê Betancourt has called, for instance, their ancestral wisdom.

The knowledge that a *mestre* gains from capoeira Angola is the product of the lineages that flow within his body. The dead *mestres* of the CAC actualize the creative potencies of being in the bodies of the living *mestres* and help them achieve bodily closure in a symbolic way. To learn about the embodiment of bodily skills is not only an initial step into the preservation of tradition, but also a further step into the spiritual and symbolic understanding of practice. In due time, a practitioner becomes aware that closing his body means more than internalizing a bodily technique. It transforms into a way of life that gives capoeira a new meaning. Although *mestres* are sometimes vague about the benefits or true meaning of the *corpo fechado*, closing the body, in essence, means an ideal to preserve power and to accumulate it. I say "an ideal" because, in the end, a *mestre* cannot live permanently with a *corpo fechado*, because he needs to relate to other beings, ask his *orixás* for protection, and risk situations of vulnerability while performing in the *rodas*.

The *corpo fechado* brings together the analytical levels of symbolism and practice. It forms a pole of intensity (Deleuze and Guatari 1987: 149–66; Viveiros de Castro 2010) that is the result of a life dedicated to understanding the consequences of openness and closure. When viewed as a pole of intensity, the *corpo fechado* executes the trick of bringing humans and nonhumans together in practice.

Notes

1. Me facão bateu em baixo
   A bananeira caiu
   Cai, cai bananeira
   A bananeira caiu.
2. Essa cobra me morde
   Senhor São Bento
   Ela é venenosa
   Senhor São Bento.
3. For a detailed account of the African discourses in capoeira, see Assunção (2005: 21–28). Concerning the Afro-centric perspective, see Desch-Obi (2000), Dossar (1992), and Thompson (1991).

CHAPTER 4

ℨ Mandinga
The Creation of Powerful Persons

It was the month of July, which meant the peak of the rainy season. It had been raining in Salvador for six weeks without reprieve. Mestre Valmir, leader of FICA Bahia, had called it a night after nobody showed up for his nightly class. The rain, unfortunately, had not encouraged people to come. As we disassembled the musical instruments and cleaned the premises, we talked about his involvement in capoeira and how he became interested in the Afro-Brazilian martial arts thanks to the charismatic presence of his teacher, Moraes, who had come from Massaranduba, which was the neighborhood in which Valmir was raised. Valmir spoke with nostalgia about his earlier years at the GCAP. He expressed his disappointment that many of the most outstanding members of the 1980s and 1990s generation had lost contact with their *mestre,* and that Moraes was not willing to make peace with many of them. Abruptly, Valmir changed the subject and started to reply to some of my earlier comments about the nature of power in capoeira. He said that I was not completely wrong about it, but that my explanation had not really grasped the meaning of that word because I did not believe truly in what *mestres* say about power and its spiritual connotations. He said, "Next Saturday in the *roda,* before it is too late, I will show you what power is."

Next Saturday, I was one of the last to arrive at the *roda.* Valmir was in a good mood, joking around and very happy to see a full house: more than thirty players were present. The *roda* went at its normal pace, with good games among all kind of practitioners. Unfortunately, because there were a lot of people that day, I did not get the opportunity to play right away. Soon, the *roda* was coming to an end and I resigned myself to being just a spectator.

Suddenly Valmir, who was playing the *atabaque* (drum similar to a conga), stopped the music, stood up, and said he wanted to play just one last game before closing the *roda*. He came toward me and said, "Sergio, this is the time." He called me to the foot of the *berimbau* (musical bow), we shook hands and sang a song. Before starting our interaction, he whispered, "I will show you what power is."

When we began to play, I felt very comfortable playing with him—very at ease. This was not an easy task, because Valmir is a very tall man and extremely dexterous. I thought for a second that I had really improved my game strategies after more than nine months practicing almost every day, three times a day. Then Valmir asked, "Are you ready?" At first I did not understand, but I felt that something in the air had changed. We went close to the music ensemble, and Valmir suddenly removed his sacred *patuás*. He said that, this time, he did not need protection. He said that he was going to show me what power really was.

I am at a loss for words to explain what happened. All my confidence collapsed, and I couldn't move. Suddenly, Valmir looked immense and I was overcome with fear. We began, but every time I started a movement, I was caught. What happened next is all a blur. I just remember vaguely the feeling in my body of kicks, a *cabeçada* in my chest and face, and four or five leg-sweeps that took me to the ground. I don't know how much time passed, but at some point Valmir stopped and said, "Enough!" The music stopped and the *roda* came to an end. I more or less regained my consciousness and started to feel pain all over my body.

Valmir had taught me a true lesson in the world of capoeira: the power of a *mestre* is real whether or not you subscribe to that power. It is concrete and something you feel in your body. It affects your well-being, your mind, and all of your senses. Its source may be spiritual, but its effects are here in the world. This inspiring but terrifying lesson of Valmir, who later apologized for his rudeness, made me wonder about reaching a concept of power that defies or goes beyond the realm of Western conceptualization.

An Ethnographic Theory of Power

How can we conceive of this non-Western theory of power based on the ethnographic context of Afro-Brazilian capoeira? If we could grasp its significance and its specificity in contrast to, or in dialogue with, the classic notions of power inherited from anthropology, how would this theory look?

In recent years different approaches have tested the limits of anthropological theory when faced with the challenge of understanding or explaining cultural diversity.[1] These approaches propose that the aim of anthropology should be to engage in thinking through ethnography, which is an inventive process that could displace our point of view about things and defy our own cultural conventions (Wagner 1981). Ethnography must not be conceived as a means to prove or discredit a preconceived idea of the world. On the contrary, it should reveal a world that tests our most rooted assumptions, to move us forward, and to create new knowledge.

Inspired by this form of ethnographic thinking, I intend to show in this chapter how a local theory of power would be perceived if anthropologists were to take the implications of an ethnographic context at face value and not as a mere representation. This does not mean withholding credit to the knowledge and cosmologies of alterity, however. The point of ethnographic writing is to make sense of others by assuming that what they say is truthful and credible, or at least plausible.

Power in capoeira is expressed by means of bodily actions that are performed by powerful persons called *mestres* or *mestras*. However, the attributes of power are considered secret: they are not transmitted systematically and their origins are vague. In capoeira Angola, power is seen and understood through practice, and by paying attention to its performative dimension. This pragmatic modality—what I will call the *antimetaphysics of power*—refers to the primacy of the empirical evidence of the body as an unquestionable proof of authority. I will develop this line of argument in more detail in the following sections.

The idea of formulating an ethnographic theory of power in anthropology is not new. One can cite antecedents in the works of Friedrich Nietzsche (1901/2011), Max Weber (1947), Marcel Mauss (2005), Michel Foucault (1980, 1988, 1999), Gilles Deleuze and Félix Guattari (1987), and Niklas Luhmann (2005). These authors have been responsible for a shift in the perception of power as a notion that resides beyond the scope of traditional political thinking.

Perhaps Marcel Mauss (2005) came the closest to devising an ethnographic theory of power. He argues that the idea of a cosmological force affecting human beings is a transcultural phenomenon that could explain reciprocity and solidarity in society (Mauss 2005: 133–37). Mauss deals mainly with a definition of power linked almost exclusively to magic, sorcery, and the unknown. Mauss's analysis is relevant because he places the notion of power beyond politics and attempts to relate it to cosmology.

However, not all anthropologists fancy the idea of using local concepts to create a theoretical framework. Those who appeal to a universal form of rationalism underlying cultural practice (Astuti and Bloch 2012; Bloch 1998, 2011; Harris 1974, 1978; Sperber 1996, 2000) do not consider it to be a fruitful venture. They consider these attempts to be misleading paths in the quest for clarity and understanding.

I disagree with universalistic approaches, mainly due to a risk of transforming cultural diversity into projections of our own making, whereby alterity is defined in terms of representations and valid (but distorted) relative worldviews. I do not claim that rationality does not exist, and believe that its importance for anthropology cannot be underestimated. However, my priority centers on cultural differences and the knowledge that we can gain from diversity that goes beyond the discourse on representation and social constructionism.

Despite skepticism among anthropologists concerning the possibility of an ethnographic theory of culture, some anthropological works have focused on the local dimension of power and have delved into its epistemic and political conditions (Anderson 1990; Arens and Karp 1989; Rapport 2003; Wagner 1986b). With different approaches, methods, and ethnographic settings, these works ponder the possibility of thinking outside Western modes of anthropological explanation and using local possibilities to create new perceptions of power.

In the following sections I examine the concept of power within capoeira Angola groups in the city of Salvador. By following practitioners in the process of learning and performing their art, I will show how an ethnographic theory of power is possible.

Performing Is Power: The Concept of *Mandinga*

Within the capoeira Angola groups in the city of Salvador there is a particular form of energy, *mandinga,* that affects emotively the lives of capoeira *mestres. Mandinga* is a cosmological force that provides knowledge, protection, and guidance to a practitioner's life. It is a modality that is recognized more explicitly in practice. *Mandinga* is not an elaborate, discursive form, but is instead about doing and seeing. It is a force manifested in the bodies of practitioners and in the dynamic of ritual interaction. In essence, *mandinga* is a form of power that capoeira leaders accumulate and display in practice. It must be noted that capoeira practitioners rarely use the word *"poder"* (power) to describe *mandinga*.

Instead, they use the words "*força*" (force) and "*energia*" (energy). Leaders of capoeira groups argue that it is advisable to avoid using *poder* in common parlance, because the word refers to the deceptive character of capoeira. They say that having power is not something to boast of. It must speak for itself in practice.

However, the attributes of *mandinga* are vague. *Mestres* consider that to talk about this concept is already an act that destines one to not understanding it. As a famous *mestre*, João Pequeno, once told me, "You will never find words to explain what is *mandinga*. There is only one way to know it—it is by doing capoeira". *Mandinga* does not need words or clear explanations; it is something one sees and experiences. It is pure, bodily evidence.

The term "*mandinga*" has scarcely been discussed in the anthropological literature on capoeira. It has been obviated (Merrel 2005; Reis 2000), tangentially addressed (Abib 2004: 190–97; Dias 2006; Vieira 1996), or completely ignored (Downey 2005; Lewis 1992). My purpose here is to describe *mandinga* in terms of the bodies and actions of the *mestres* and to discuss the consequences of such embodiment in the expression of power relations and social formations.

Mandinga becomes visible through bodily acts of deception and trickery that form the core logic of practice in capoeira. Those acts are the foundations of the attributes of a *mestre*'s power. Trickery, deception, and cunning play a substantial role in the definition of shrewdness, which is expressed in other social practices in Brazil. Roberto DaMatta (1991) identified deception as the quintessential skill of the *malandro*, which is the morally ambiguous character in Brazilian society who is the equivalent of a trickster—one who plays simultaneously with good and evil.

A capoeira player is a *malandro* who needs to embody deception not only as a virtue, but also as a form of accessing power. Although the two words have similar means, I would like to make a distinction between *malandro* and *mandinga* in this chapter. The former I relate to the general realm of deceptive cultural skills that are not exclusive to capoeira. The latter encompasses the attributes of the *malandro*, but has a particular significance in the fact that it is the primary source of power in capoeira.

The exact meaning of *mandinga* is difficult for anthropologists to understand. In a recent documentary by Lázaro Faria (2005), some of the most important *mestres* give their opinions concerning the deceptive character of this concept and its apparent ineffability. Here are some of their answers:

> *Mandinga* is something a player is lucky to be born with [Mestre Alabama]. ... *Mandinga* is the knowledge of the invisible [Mestre Bola Sete]. ... *Mandinga* is the soul of the game [Mestre Camisa]. ... *Mandinga* is the enticement of capoeira. It is the permanent lie; it is the intangibility of a capoeira player that looks like magic [Mestre Decanio]. ... *Mandinga* is to know how to live, how to make much out of nothing; it is knowing how to get in and out of situations [Mestre Cobra Mansa]. ... [*Mandinga*] is a trick, it is to pretend; it is digging into your tooth until blood spits out so that you can claim that you have a toothache [Mestre Gigante]. (Faria 2005, my translation and my transcription)

Mandinga seems to have contrasting meanings among capoeira experts. While it was fairly easy to define the *corpo fechado* discussed in chapter 3, it has been difficult to find out what *mandinga* is and to truly understand it. However, as I mentioned before, *mestres* all agree that it is deceptive in character. It is the ultimate act of simulation and trickery that embodies the attributes of the *malandro*.

Although *mestres* hold cosmological notions about the nature of power that are similar to those of the Javanese people studied by Anderson (1990), these notions differ mainly in the character of accumulation of energy and in the meaningful expression of the word "power." *Mandinga* becomes real only when it is performed. Practice is the only way to prove that a *mestre* is a powerful subject.[2]

I would like to emphasize that what makes this ethnographic notion of power relevant from an anthropological perspective is its anti-essentialism—its refusal to stand as an elaborate transcendental form. This brings us back to the deceptive character of capoeira practitioners. If power exists, it is in action, through bodily performance (as I have shown in the vignette at the beginning of the chapter). The materiality of the body becomes power as one acts and moves in deceptive ways. In other words, the force of the *mandinga*, having merged with the body of a practitioner, makes social transcendence impossible.

This means that a good capoeira practitioner, one who gains power, is a person who learns how to cheat and betray an adversary in order to succeed. During the early stage of my research in Salvador in 2005, following a daily lesson in Mestre Boca do Rio's capoeira academy, Mestre Boca do Rio mentioned, "*Mandinga* is the capacity of deceiving an adversary. It is to play without being caught open or exposed. It is to pretend that I am going to get away from the *roda* [capoeira circle] and suddenly come back with an attack. It is to smile, although I am full of fear or anger. It consists always in keeping things hidden—and protected." This view is also shared by Mestre João Pequeno, one of the founders of modern capoeira Angola, who explains in Faria's (2005) documentary: "*Mandinga* is to pretend that you are going to make a move, but you don't, and when he [the opponent] least expects it, then you move" (2005, my translation and my transcription).

Mandinga looks, at first glance, like something that one uses exclusively when practicing capoeira. One might think of it solely as a bodily technique that a practitioner assimilates. This is the interpretation of the process of learning capoeira that Greg Downey, for instance, offers. For Downey (2008: 206), learning would fundamentally take place in an imitative way, in a process of scaffolding that includes partial imitations, coaching, and verbal explanations. Although I agree in principle with Downey, I consider that the analysis could be expanded to a domain beyond the bodily techniques of the game. For instance, Mestre Valmir, the leader of the FICA in Bahia and another of my informants, believes that teaching *mandinga* as a technique is impossible, even though *mandinga* is the key to understanding capoeira. He says, "*Mandinga* is something very complicated to talk about. It is the secret of capoeira. I cannot teach it and transmit it to anybody. It is a thing that a student must discover by himself. It has nothing to do with technique. It helps, but *mandinga* comes from somewhere else. It is a mystery, but it is real. You can see it in the game and in the behavior of some *mestres*. *Mandinga* is what makes and defines a *mestre*."

Other practitioners offer similar statements regarding the impossibility of teaching *mandinga* in the classroom. For instance, Contramestre Electricista mentions, "You do not teach *mandinga*, you learn it" (Abib 2004: 103). However, of the *mestres* I interviewed in Salvador, not even one would describe with precision the process of learning *mandinga*. In general, they gave elusive answers, pointing out that acquiring *mandinga* was an individual quest that could not rely on the transmission of knowledge from *mestre* to student. I concluded that *mandinga* consists of more than a just set of bodily techniques that can be taught, as Downey claims. Rather, *mandinga* must be understood as a discovery that a *mestre* first unveils and that later is embodied without another person's help.

To conceive of *mandinga* as something that is innate provides an argument in favor of predestination. If only the chosen ones are able to obtain it, the impossibility of teaching *mandinga* mirrors the situation experienced when describing past heroic feats, epic battles, or even modern Herculean efforts displayed by athletes. If *mandinga* is conceived as the secret of capoeira, it is because nobody can define it exactly, although they can see it in action. It is expressed in the bodies of practitioners but their learning is something nobody can explain, therefore it has an apparently predestined character.

While a categorical answer to the question of the characteristics and appropriation of *mandinga* has eluded me, it is possible to analyze the individual prowess of practitioners by focusing on the social and supernatural repercussions of *mandinga*.

Evidence: Supernatural Acts and the Relevance of Music

Bodily techniques do not seem adequate to explain the nature of *mandinga*. It is necessary to look for answers not in the ambit of game strategies, but rather (much as in the case of the *corpo fechado*) in the spiritual and religious domain of the Afro-Brazilian religion of Candomblé. As I have mentioned in previous chapters, Candomblé has a considerable influence in capoeira.

Downey (2005: 138) has highlighted the existing relationship between these two practices: "Some suggest that a concept of an 'open body' originated in African religion or magic and helped to generate closure practices in both capoeira and Candomblé, making the two part of a single cultural complex." While he hints that there are spiritual connotations in the concept of the *corpo fechado*, he did not pursue them in his research. He indicates there are similarities and connections between capoeira and Candomblé, but he does not promote either one as a unifying practice: "When capoeiristas turn to Candomblé (as many do) they often draw on religious resources out of the physical sense of danger instilled by capoeira, rather than any logic internal to Candomblé. They sample Candomblé as one in a diverse repertoire of defensive maneuvers, using ritual, religious practice, and magic as they would capoeira techniques" (ibid.: 147).

While I agree with Downey's analysis of Candomblé as another defensive technique for beginners and for some intermediate and advanced students of capoeira, it is possible to see Candomblé not only as a game strategy but also as a way of being that permeates the life of a *mestre*. As I have shown in chapter 3, Candomblé is not strictly a technique; it is essentially a religion that has a strong influence on capoeira. As Mestre Valmir mentions: "Candomblé is the religion of capoeira, and one cannot separate them. They are necessarily interconnected."

Therefore, important notions of Candomblé, such as *axé* and *dendé*, which refer to conceptions of energy like those described by Mauss about *mana*, have become common parlance among capoeira practitioners. *Mestres* often consider a good *roda* or a good game as having a good *axé*. However, *axé*, *dendé*, and *mandinga* are not synonymous terms. *Axé* is a cosmic energy that impregnates all life; it is the substance that forms *orixás* and all beings in the world. *Mandinga* is a subcategory of *axé* that is molded exclusively for capoeira, while *dendé* is a type of *axé* that materializes in palm oil, which is used in Candomblé to cook ritual meals. One could say that while *mandinga* describes a certain kind of *axé*, *axé* does not necessarily involve *mandinga*.

The concept of *mandinga* is located at a crossroads between bodily actions and the precepts of Candomblé. There is a complementarity between the two domains: they are parts of a plural cosmology, but it is difficult to separate their particular influence in practice. For instance, *mestres* will state that *mandinga* borrows some aspects from Candomblé but does not come from Candomblé—that it is external to the precepts of the Afro-Brazilian religion. This is why *mestres* who have adopted other religious views can still talk about and believe in the power of *mandinga*.

Power becomes evident in what *mestres* call supernatural acts. Such acts define a person as powerful and establish the antimetaphysics of power as an ineffable proof. In order to release the power of their *mandinga*, *mestres* must follow certain procedures before and during a *roda*. Most of these procedures involve restrictions and taboos similar to those found in Candomblé, and they are designed to close the body. Some of the prerequisites before the *roda* include sexual abstinence, avoidance of certain types of food, and purifying showers with special herbal concoctions. As I mentioned in the previous chapter, the main source of bodily protection during the *roda* is the donning of amulets and particular types of colored clothes, accompanied by singing songs dedicated to the *orixás*.

There are more elements that help to achieve a *corpo fechado*, but the aforementioned practices are the most important. They give extra protection to a *mestre,* especially when he is playing against more-experienced *mestres,* or in situations where he is challenged by a hostile adversary. Protective measures augment the strength of a *mestre* and help him to effectively release his *mandinga.*

Some of the proofs of *mandinga* are manifested in fascinating and smooth acrobatic movements, which include playful, deceptive body and facial gestures as well as unpredictable subtle attacks. When one is said to have *mandinga,* he or she is moving loosely and lightly—not necessarily fast, but aesthetically nimble. At the same time, the person who is embodying *mandinga* looks as if he is possessed. According to my informants, the intensity of a game can lead to supernatural feats that serve as evidence of their power. For instance, they claim that their *mandinga* makes them bigger and more physically immense in a *roda.* They can paralyze opponents by looking at them and instilling fear in their hearts. They act as if they have animal powers (from crocodiles and snakes) and can predict movements, visualize positions of vulnerability, and steal or diminish the power of another person.

Many of the procedures that take place prior to a *roda* are designed to protect not only the body of a player but also his *mandinga.* Because *mestres* can steal one another's *mandinga* in a game, it is necessary to defend it at all costs. Protection of *mandinga* becomes an obsession, as Downey (2005: 153–68) has described in a chapter aptly titled "Walking in Evil." The *mestres'* quasi-paranoid attitude and awareness of constantly being under attack demands cautious behavior from a *mestre* in almost everything he does. It is not by chance that this behavior resonates with the plural cosmology of Candomblé, in which similar beliefs exist and in which protection is paramount.

Despite the protection provided by *patuás,* practitioners may still inflict an injury on an opponent in a *roda* by using astute contrivances. In this respect, Mestre Boca do Rio says,

> You need to come protected to the *roda* because you do not know what is going to happen. ... A person can take away your energy simply by looking at you. You will think, "This man plays a lot!" What you do not know is that this person is taking all the energy away from you. And then you will get out of the *roda* feeling as if someone had just beaten you, thinking: "Damn, I could not play today! He did not give me a chance!" You will feel tired as if you had trained all week without rest. This is the game! Therefore, you have to carry your *patuás* with you at all times in order to have protection. I have never seen, in a *roda* of capoeira Angola, a *mestre* without *patuás.* Look around and you will

perceive everybody coming with *patuás* on their neck or in their pockets. A real capoeira player never comes by chance to a *roda;* he needs to know what he is doing there.

The expression of one's *mandinga* is enacted by using bodily movements that *mestres* define as deceptive, such as touching the ground with the hands, shaking abruptly the whole upper body, and smiling constantly. In other cases, *mandinga* becomes visible when a player puts his or her adversary on the ground by artful means. The quality of the enactment of *mandinga* sets apart the *mestres* from other practitioners of capoeira Angola. While a player might grasp the effects of *mandinga,* *mestres* believe that it is impossible for beginners or advanced students with just a few years of experience to achieve a high level of sophistication when applying deceptive moves, because they still have not understood how to use and control *mandinga* in their bodies.

The mastery of *mandinga* thus sets apart a *mestre* from the rest of his practitioners. This could explain the sparse number of *mestres* and *contramestres* of capoeira Angola in Salvador. Because their power is exclusively a matter of predestination, individual discovery, and persistence through time, it is no wonder that individuals can receive the title only after many years, or even decades, of practice. This lengthy apprenticeship process keeps a stable ratio of a few *mestres* and *contramestres* at the top of the hierarchy: around thirty had registered capoeira groups in Salvador in the years 2005–6 and an additional twenty did not have groups. The number has exponentially proliferated since then, however. In addition, there is an increasing population of local students who form the core of every one of the twenty academies at that time in the city, with every academy having at least ten students.

In the capoeira practitioner's quest for power and self-control, music plays an important role in the comprehension of the spiritual domain of power due to its magic and playful connotations in performance. *Mestres* pay close attention to every element in the music ensemble. The *bateria* (ensemble) consists of eight instruments: two *pandeiros* (tambourines), an *atabaque,* an *agogô* (a double-bell), a *reco-reco* (scrapper), and three *berimbaus* (resonance instruments): the *gunga, medio,* and *viola.* These last are the most important instruments of the ensemble. Made of the *beriba* tree, the *berimbau* consists of a stick approximately one and a half meters long, an *arame* (steel wire), a *cabaça* (gourd), and a *caxixi* (rattle). When assembled, the *berimbau* has a shape like that of a bow, due to the arched tension produced by the steel string attached at both ends of the wooden stick.

The three *berimbaus* form the core of the music orchestra. *Mestres* view these instruments as the caretakers of capoeira. *Berimbaus* are perceived to be persons (see chapter 6 for a full description); they are subjects that speak to guide bodily actions. Their sound is very loud and hollow. In the *roda*, *berimbaus* send warning messages to the players and summon somebody to attack an opponent. When a *mestre* plays a *berimbau*, he is transmitting his *mandinga* to the instrument. He can make the instrument speak louder and even cry out. *Mestres* say that what occurs is a fusion as the instrument and their bodies become one in the performances. Therefore, a *berimbau* has an agency and it can contain part of the *mandinga* of a *mestre*. That is why only *mestres, contramestres,* and advanced students are allowed to play a *berimbau* in a *roda*. The rest of the practitioners can play any of the other instruments, but never the *berimbaus*.

Mestres say that listening to a *berimbau* is also a way to hear the *mandinga* of a player. The materiality of sounds serves as proof of power and motivates the bodily expression of its practitioners; it affects practitioners emotively, enhancing their awareness of danger and vulnerability, it also foments action and courage in a person.

However, capoeira Angola music is composed of more than instrumentals; the repertoire includes songs with lyrics, some of which refer to the existence of *mandinga*. For instance:

> I do not give my *mandinga* to anybody
> I do not give it to anybody,
> I do not give it to anybody,
> I do not give my *mandinga* to anybody.[3]

Music and songs are thus embedded within the logic of capoeira in such a way that they represent another expression of *mandinga*. What is of paramount importance for *mestres* is that the evidence and the materialization of power in their bodies or in their objects or sounds is made clear to other practitioners in the hierarchy of power.

Deception and Powerful Persons

The expression of *mandinga* is inherently an intimate act that produces substantial and irreversible changes. The discovery of *mandinga* is what transforms a person into a *mestre* and makes him a powerful subject. This discovery could be confirmed by other practitioners when they perceive the individualistic or subjective connotations of the concept itself. While a dexterous, advanced player is sometimes considered a *mandingueiro* (someone who embodies *mandinga*), the fact that he can deceive and use streetwise strategies to open bodies during a game does not mean that he is a *mestre*. In order to become a *mestre*, one needs to have control and a full consciousness of *mandinga*. In fact, when leaders see a practitioner playing with shrewdness and cunning, they talk more in terms of *malandragem* (DaMatta 1991). Furthermore, as I have explained earlier, the attributes of the *malandro* are part of Brazilian society as a whole—it is not a term that can be applied exclusively to capoeira practitioners.

The exclusiveness of *mandinga* acts as the extrapolation of a *mestre's* subjectivity. It sets apart a group of chosen persons from the rest and bestows legitimacy on the *mestres*. While *mestres* consider the process of discovering *mandinga* to be a secret or as an ineffable truth (it simply happens, with no explanation as to how or why), such discovery produces an ideal identification among *mestres*. It works as a moment of revelation regarding the deceptive quality of the world. In this sense, the attributes of power form part of the general plural cosmology that encompasses other aspects of Afro-Brazilian culture and extends to the ontological perception of the environment.

Deception stands at the core of the perceptual world. For *mestres*, humanity possesses a "negative capability" (Stoller 1989: 144; Wagner 2001) to deceive. By performing deception efficiently, humans become powerful, in part because they can more easily see the real intentions of other humans.

There are no collective rituals for an initiation into *mandinga*. *Mestres* explain that *mandinga* is a personal discovery, experienced individually. It happens exactly when a person is ready; it is an infallible but unpredictable event. When a practitioner discovers *mandinga*, other *mestres* can see it and even neophytes can feel it with an immediate, indisputable recognition.

Mandinga transforms an individual into a *mestre*—a powerful person. A *mestre* shows many similar attributes to the charismatic person studied by Weber (1947) and Geertz (1993: 121–146) and to the " Poor Man, Rich Man, Big Man, Chief" of Polynesia and Melanesia analyzed by Sahlins (1963), Andrew Strathern (2007), and Godelier (1986). He represents the community of participants, embodies the desirable attributes of deception and knowledge, and is the supreme authority in his academy.

One of the direct effects of charismatic power in capoeira is the creation of pyramidal hierarchies in which *mestres* exercise their authority vertically and arbitrarily. The power that these individuals discover and accumulate in the *roda* also extends to the realm of mundane social relations. *Mandinga* absorbs and models interactions among practitioners beyond the limits imposed by capoeira. The dictates that guide deceptive actions, along with seductive cunning and artful strategies, mark the asymmetrical relationship between leaders and students. Therefore, it is not by chance that secrecy and protection of the body become second nature among *mestres*. Once an individual gains the power of *mandinga,* any friend or acquaintance could be a potential enemy willing to betray or to steal that power. In this respect, *mandinga* leads to an attitude of deference and respect, similar to the attitudes found in Candomblé where the act of distancing oneself from others in the process of learning is a common practice, because it requires that knowledge be something that one must obtain through artful means, without asking too many questions (Goldman 2008).

Thus, alterity becomes a risk to any enterprise (such as capoeira and Candomblé) that strives to establish a definitive asymmetrical relationship of power. In the case of capoeira, alterity bears the seeds of uncertainty, because no *mestre* can be completely sure about the real intentions of others and can lose his power if he falls into another's trap. With no other resources at hand, a *mestre* must rely on his personal *mandinga* and the strength of his *corpo fechado* to face an uncertain world.

The Ontology of Deception as the Foundation of Power

The ethnographic material on the concept of power in capoeira Angola isolates seven main characteristics of that power. The first is that power comes from an unknown and ambiguous source (an unclear form of *axé*). The second is that power is visible only in its performance (locally referred as *mandinga*) and its manifestation in the body. The third is that this manifestation is always deceptive: power, in this sense, is always masked. The fourth is that power is cumulative, but it must be performed or demonstrated to become real. The fifth is that power cannot be transmitted or taught; it is discovered after many years or even decades of persistent practice. The sixth is that power privileges certain individuals, called *mestres,* who are responsible for the transmission of knowledge and the continuation of tradition in capoeira. The seventh and last characteristic is that the power shapes social relations through deception.

One may wonder if it is possible to construct a theory of power based on the ethnography of capoeira. I believe that it is possible to do so if one takes deception and trickery as its foundation. So far, I have obviated these two terms: "deception" and "trickery." They were expressions of *mandinga* and provided proof of its existence. However, it is necessary to return to these two concepts and delve into their ontological connotations, if one wants to understand the relationship between social norms and playful individual action.

For capoeira practitioners, deception is a negative capability that they attempt to master through an endless process of learning and experiencing in order to see through the world in which they live. For *mestres,* deception is a form of life. There is, apparently, no morality in it; it only exists and is something that they perform. This explains why outsiders are perplexed when they try to project ethical attributes onto the *mestres,* because *mestres* are not interested in becoming moral figures.

The term "deception" has ontological implications. How does one conceive of sociality when deception is a mode of being? Certainly, the word implies a connotation of masking—in this case, masking power. Capoeira *mestres* explain that power cannot be expressed literally but rather through artful means that wrap it in humor, ambiguity, and secrecy. *Mandinga* develops as a form of learning or discovery that becomes second nature—a nature that is contradictory and perplexing and exists only in appearance. This is another way of explaining the quasi-paranoid attitudes of *mestres* and perhaps of all Candomblé devotees. A world of appearances is always deceptive in nature; if one is constantly facing a world without transcendence, then there is always a probability that one can be tricked or deceived. However, this probability is another reason to take deception humorously, as a form of joking. *Mestres* are, in this sense, tricksters, individuals who play with social rules, using them to their own convenience in, apparently, nonserious ways. This is the core of deception for them, to take lightly the human seriousness of life even if everything they deem valuable is at stake.

If *mestres* can see through deception and know what they perceive behind the world of appearances, they will not share what they've seen with us; they will remain silent. This is another form of protecting the secret of *mandinga.*

Much as in the world of thieves described by Italo Calvino (1995), where everybody steals and cheats as a way of life, honesty is a hindrance in the world of capoeira. Honesty (or our concept of honesty) cannot be considered a quality of power among *mestres,* because it would leave their real intentions and their power exposed. The ontology of deception in capoeira would advise the opposite: wrap, feign, pretend, seduce, play, and trick others. Perhaps, as *mestres* of capoeira assume, the whole world does indeed move through the guise of deception. One may be tempted to generalize this concept to create a feasible theory of power that can provide tools for comparison and allow one to explore the roles of masking and simulation within social power dynamics.

Notes

1. Among these approaches, we can mention the works of Arens and Karp 1989; Holbraad 2008b, 2012; Karp and Masolo 2000; Strathern 1990, 2004; Viveiros de Castro 1998, 2004, 2010; Wagner 1972, 1981, 1991; and Weiner 1988.
2. For a similar view on the performative character of power, see Freeman (2007).
3. Minha mandinga eu não dou pra ninguém
   Não dou pra ninguém, não dou pra ninguém
   Minha mandinga eu não dou pra ninguém.

CHAPTER 5

ꙮ Playful Violence and the Ambiguity of Deception

The logic of capoeira Angola is based on deception and the symbolic and cosmological connotation of embodied action. It also involves the historical and sociological agency of powerful persons. These are elements that provide capoeira with a pragmatic force that interconnects different levels of culture. This chapter analyses the effects of the pragmatics of capoeira within the scope of a moral[1] dilemma among three concepts: playfulness, deception, and violence. As I have mentioned in previous chapters, the importance to capoeira of cunning, betrayal, and artfulness poses some questions about the apparent lack of moral principles in *mestres'* attitudes. If the power of misleading is considered to be the ultimate indicator of skill in capoeira, is it possible to discuss an ethical framework in capoeira Angola? Furthermore, how do leaders deal with the contradictory pragmatics of capoeira? This chapter addresses these issues by paying attention to the philosophical and ambiguous nature of capoeira. Any philosophical reflection about capoeira Angola emerges from the conundrum posited among playfulness, deception, and violence.

What Is Capoeira, After All?

Mestres define capoeira Angola as an inherently ambiguous practice. Capoeira's norms are contradictory when executed, and the reliance on deception and playfulness always brings unexpected outcomes. For example, anthropologist Greg Downey followed Geertz's assumption and classified capoeira as a blurred genre that combines a different set of cultural characteristics like ritual, martial art, dance, and sometimes sportive competition (Downey 2002: 490). Because capoeira is defined simultaneously as a combination of these cultural characteristics, leaders mention that it may elude any attempt of classification. One must bear in mind that this does not necessarily mean that capoeira consists simply in a joyfully free experiential engagement or in a violent combative confrontation. Capoeira is more than this. It is an amalgamation of elements acting as parts of a whole. Much like other martial arts, like karate and kung fu, capoeira Angola is conceived as a way of life that encompasses a holistic worldview. Leaders say that capoeira transcends the individual; it is everything the mouth can eat, as Mestre Pastinha used to say.

The ludic aspects of the Angola style combined with its symbolic violent expressions seem to bring a set of irresolvable contradictions between conventional norms dictated by the seriousness of capoeira and the individual playful creation of free action. There is no synthesis, apparently, that can solve the conundrum between playfulness and violence. Nevertheless, there have been attempts to overcome the difficulties about the essence of capoeira, which will be explored later in the chapter.

The next section focuses on the aspects of playing and fighting—how they appear in practice, and how practitioners interpret them. I include some ethnographic descriptions of bouts in which the ambiguity between playfulness and violence creates a persistent tension in the existing rules; this tension evinces some of the most characteristic dilemmas for practitioners in their process of apprenticeship.

Playful Violence in Practice

Whatever is meaningful or important in the practice of capoeira Angola must be shown within the boundaries of the *roda,* in which the physical expression of the practice takes full form. *Mestres* say that one of the most recurrent explanations of the combat situation in capoeira is that it is a martial art-dance-fight. Bodies move nimbly to music with the goal of deceiving an opponent. Practitioners use graceful bodily gestures, attacks, and counterattacks, and must be aware of the exposures of the *corpo fechado.* They also need to protect their own *mandinga,* or show it when necessary.

Mestres and advanced students, for instance, are known to anticipate the movements of their adversaries in order to manipulate them into exposing, or opening, their bodies. Experienced players will show control in their moves and will refrain from expressing any symptom of annoyance if another player tries to kick violently or displays attacks in an aggressive way. Experienced players will continue to use acrobatic escapes against such kicks with smiles on their faces to calm down the stressed opponent.

Violence, nevertheless, is always latent in capoeira Angola no matter the gender of the players.[2] It is part of the practice's history, but it appears in a disguised form. Because capoeira consists of hidden intentions of violence, players cannot show openly their real states of mind. It would go against the mandates of the *corpo fechado* and the self-preservation of *mandinga*.

Mestres maintain that capoeira Angola is the *arte de lutar sorrindo* (the art of fighting with a smile). Although this ideal is highly praised, practitioners do not always follow it. I witnessed many bouts in which a player clearly lost his temper and forgot that he was only there to simulate violence. I experienced moments when rage took over the spirit of the *roda*. Players lost their teeth, had their noses broken, were kicked in the head, and earned bruises all over their bodies. Capoeira Angola practitioners sometimes mean serious business. In the 1940s Mestre Pastinha said that capoeira was an art for *valentões* (tough guys). Nowadays, that spirit is still alive, although it is contained or disguised.

It is the *mestres'* job to keep a *roda* amicable. Although there are no clear rules about what to do when an aggressive practitioner appears, the first inclination is to calm him down. In order to achieve this, the *mestre* in charge will call him close to the music ensemble and give some words of admonition or end the interaction immediately. The decision depends on who is playing. If the practitioners are beginners, *mestres* will stop the interaction. If they are advanced students, the interaction will continue until it is clear who is capable of opening a body in the best way. Finally, if the practitioners are *mestres*, they decide when to call it off. The tolerance to violence depends on the hierarchy of power.

Rodas of capoeira Angola may last between two and five hours. Every *roda* that I witnessed in Salvador was recognized according to the practitioners who visited it. Some *rodas* were considered to be dangerous, while other were considered to be mild, and everything in between. In principle, most performances welcome any capoeira practitioner of any style, although not everybody attends the same *rodas*. *Mestres* often recommended avoiding certain *rodas* and certain *mestres* as a cautionary measure.

The involvement in the culture of capoeira affects the daily lives of practitioners, particularly their assumption about violence, and their perception of danger. *Mestres* always warn that capoeira is a holistic practice, and that one learns lessons in the *roda* or the classroom that will affect their conduct and perception of the world at large.

Similar interpretations of the influence between a bodily practice and daily life appear in the practice of aikido. According to Tamara Kohn, certain attitudes and feelings in people practicing aikido extend to life outside the dojo. She says, "Nearly all of these people who train [aikido] for any length of time, however, will eventually come to understand their practice in terms of a number of key principles of movement that are very commonly related to analogous reactions and events in their everyday social world" (Kohn 2003: 144). The influence that capoeira Angola has in the life of practitioners is transformative and long lasting. Capoeira instill into players the attitudes of deception beyond the scope of the *roda*, and set up a set of ambiguous moral principles to guide their lives.

The logic of deception and the quest for power influence capoeira's apparent lack of ethics. This presumed lack, which appears contradictory to an outsider, does not perplex practitioners; it is understood to be a part of the lessons that capoeira teaches to students. I will return to the apparently nonethics of capoeira Angola in a moment. First, though, it is necessary for the discussion to describe briefly how capoeira players understand the relationship between social norms and playful action in the *roda*.

Bending the Rules

As Greg Downey (2005: 24) has argued, the focus on deception removes any pretension to fair play in capoeira Angola bouts. *Mestres* praise practitioners' abilities to create attacks from a disguised position in a way that addresses the vulnerabilities of an opponent. Such attacks are viewed as latent dangerous possibilities. For instance, during a bout a *mestre* might go down to the floor feigning an injury following an opponent's leg-sweep, only to surprise his opponent with a quick *cabeçada* when the practitioner comes closer with an open guard to give support to the seemingly injured *mestre*. A *mestre* can also interact with the audience in order to distract his opponent. I have seen practitioners falling into the trap of distraction, and ending up on the floor by means of an unexpected attack.

Mestre Curió is considered the master of deception in Salvador. He has feigned an injury and then thrown an opponent out of the *roda* with a *cabeçada*, called a woman from the audience to the *roda* to ask for her protection against a "violent" player, and withdrawn a hidden pocket knife and threatened an opponent who almost "got him" with a leg-sweep. He makes a variety of expressions with his face, shouts to the public, and implements constant pauses in the *roda* just to distract his opponents. Many players consider Curió to be the most dangerous of all capoeira *mestres* because he has the most unexpected resources at hand. He is the embodiment of deception and, although he is now almost eighty years old, his capacity to surprise opponents is still intact.

These acts of simulation and deception contrast with the usual ethics of sports and oriental martial arts. For instance, nobody would praise a marathon runner who uses a shortcut. Athletes who bend the rules to their own benefit in other sports are sure to be sanctioned. In capoeira Angola, however, the opposite is true. The rules are bent depending on the interest and status of a practitioner. A *mestre*, for instance, might manipulate and break an implicit rule, like slapping the face of an opponent, but only if he manages to do so by disguising his intentions to later inflict a legal attack. In the same manner, he can appeal to his condition of power when he bends the rules to act violently, explaining later that he knew he was using his energy in a very intimidating way but that, ultimately, he was the *mestre* and was allowed to do so because his prestige was at stake.

Many local capoeira practitioners are familiar with the attitudes toward deception and bending the rules. These attitudes are an extension of their daily lives in the streets of Salvador, and a result of their daily engagement with a world in which negotiation with hustlers and rogues is common and confrontations with a repressive society is constant. *Mestres* go as far as to venture that the origins of this attitude reside in the history of slavery. They maintain that capoeira was a consequence of the deceptive occult acts of slaves. The oppressive situation lived by slaves in Brazil made them act always with care and suspicion before their masters, so they had to learn to negotiate in order to survive. Thus, deception became a kind of power of the weak, a strategy that was used to counterattack the absolute power that was exercised over them. *Mestres* believe that the social situation of Afro-Brazilians has not changed much since then, and that Afro-Brazilians must be deceptive to achieve recognition that will allow them to fight against the powers of the elites. In a sense the practice of capoeira praises deception not only as a means of survival, but also as an expression of supreme ability for Afro-Brazilians to fight against injustice and discrimination.

In institutionalized sports, the fair bending of rules is either minimal or nonexistent. Rather, a clear body of rules prevails, and usually there are referees whose duty is to supervise the correct implementation of the rules. In capoeira Angola, there are no written laws or codes of conduct: undesirable acts are sanctioned according to the criteria of the *mestres*. In this sense, a *mestre* is the judge of actions in a *roda* and subjectively determines the limits of rule bending.

The Ethical Approach of Mestre Pastinha

Local approaches to understand the philosophical principles of capoeira Angola became popularized in the writings of Mestre Pastinha. He was and still is the main source of philosophical thought about capoeira, according to almost all *mestres* in Salvador, Bahia. Mestre Decanio said, "Pastinha was the first capoeira Angola player who analyzed capoeira as a philosophy and who was concerned about the ethical and educational aspects of its practice" (Decanio 1997: 5). As a result, Pastinha introduced a new way of perceiving capoeira Angola.[3]

Pastinha worried about the apparent contradictions between playfulness and violence in capoeira. He was aware that the process of institutionalizing capoeira Angola had to address this issue in order to legitimatize it as a formal practice, and made an effort to outline a theory of practice. Unfortunately, he was never known for clarity in giving explanations, and many of his answers to topics connected with the essence of the game and the rules involved were obscure and full of parables and enigmatic statements. He blended lessons of ethics with mystical explanations and philosophical concerns about the world. For him, Capoeira was too complex to understand fully. It shone with a spiritual aura that was not easy to grasp for a practitioner. However, he believed that the key to finding a comprehensive explanation of the full meaning of capoeira resided in observing and meditating about the logic of the game in the *roda*. This is why he dedicated great part of his manuscript to describe situations related to bodily sequences, escapes, defensive movements, and deceptive attacks. For him, a practitioner had to internalize the complex relation between playful and violence, he said that a student should, in the first instance, internalize his energy, which is the source of control over the game: "In the practice of this science, my friends, you do not know what you have in yourself, if it belongs to you, or if nature gave it to you, try to perfection it. Trust in yourself, love your sport and not egoism, discover that truth is an endless fight, in sum, a general and abstract definition, which characterizes every existence, every being" (Decanio 1997: 19).

This quote evokes a kind of energy, perhaps *axé* or *mandinga*, that constitutes the truth of the world and that can be mastered by capoeira practitioners through self-control or proper use of capoeira knowledge. Because Pastinha referred to capoeira as a science, we can infer that he considered its practice to be a form of knowledge about the world. However, what is important is that he acknowledges the struggles that any practitioner faces when dealing with a bodily interaction that demands a possible violent situation and a playfully controlled response.

Pastinha argued that understanding the essence of capoeira would help a practitioner to overcome the conundrum between playfulness and violence by appealing to a specific code of conduct. This understanding depended on the assimilation of a moral scope that existed deep in the logic of practice but that was not apparent to beginners or advanced players but nevertheless helped them to achieve control of their actions. He says, "A good capoeira player never gets excited or exalted; he always tries to be calm in order to react with precision and accuracy. He does not argue with his comrades and students, he does not attack in the game without reason, just to annoy his comrades and hence start a brawl. He teaches his students without boasting himself in an aggressive way and without introducing himself indecorously" (Decanio 1997: 23). Pastinha considered an ethical code to be essential in order to avoid open confrontations between practitioners. He concludes that the elements of playfulness and violence must therefore be regulated: "Unfortunately, the majority of capoeira players have just a partial knowledge of capoeira rules. It is the control of the game that protects practitioners from falling into an excess of *vale tudo* [lawless fight], but listen, I am talking in the sense of showing [control] and not of defiance, this last aspect always brings disastrous consequences. It takes away all the beauty and brilliance from capoeira, and in this manner, a player may lose, pointlessly, his capacities" (Decanio 1997: 27).

Pastinha's emphasis on using an ethical code to regulate the practice of capoeira Angola was part of his effort to strip away its association with a violent past, and with the kind of capoeira played in the streets and at festivals. Pastinha mentioned that control and self-transformation was the ethical aspiration of any student who was always tempted by the "evil" or dark side of capoeira.

When *mestres* reflect on the legacy of Mestre Pastinha today, they agree with his goal to find a balance between the artistic, playful side of capoeira and its violent, fighting principles. Whatever his real intentions, the core of Pastinha's teachings addressed the conundrum that practitioners encountered during their apprenticeship. If he wanted to regulate and change the way one should behave, it is because he knew that the path of survival for the coming generations was by means of institutionalization; his was a project for the future. If he wanted to introduce changes, it was perhaps because he saw that things were going in the opposite direction and wanted to distance the future of capoeira from its past association with tough guys and troublemakers.

Pastinha's reflections were the first written theorizations about capoeira Angola. His manuscript was the first attempt to find an alternative to the dilemma between playfulness and violence. His ethical concerns were a form to solve the puzzle of a practice that was not only an art of self-defense that could be dangerous, violent, and treacherous, but also a playful, aesthetic practice with ritual and cosmological connotations. However, his ethical ideal set the bar too high for other capoeira practitioners of the period. In the next section, I look at other contemporary alternatives to the problem of playfulness and violence in capoeira. I describe how the initial ethical dimension settled by Mestre Pastinha was transformed into a complex mixture of opposite attitudes and values that consolidated the present vision of the martial art and gave rise to a heightened image of other important elements, like trickery, malice, and roguery.

Malícia and *Manha*

The ethical code implemented by Mestre Pastinha was not completely accepted by other capoeira *mestres*. It has been more than fifty years since Pastinha introduced his teachings, and they are viewed more as ideals—the highest appeal to self-conduct and self-restraint that one can achieve through capoeira—than as actual guidelines. Most capoeira players of the time did not follow Pastinha's recommendations. The narratives, and the culture of capoeira in general, include a mixture of ambiguous attitudes toward the martial art. In the following pages, I illustrate some examples of how players deal with the apparent contradictions between playfulness and violence by referring to the uses of three concepts that will be defined shortly: *malícia* (malice), *manha* (trickery), and *malandragem* (roguery).

The first example comes from the book *History and Stories of Capoeira* by Jose Oliveira Cruz (2006), who is also known as Mestre Bola Sete. A student of Mestre Pastinha, Oliveira describes in this story how he came to hear about famous capoeira practitioners and the way they learned or used capoeira as a method of dealing with dangerous social situations. Partly based on anecdotes and partly on his own experiences as a *mestre*, the narrative of Oliveira Cruz is rich in examples of how capoeira players lived their lives dangerously in the streets of Salvador in the period between 1940 and 1970.

From the rich and varied anecdotes found in the book, I choose one about the violent behavior of a practitioner named Raymundo Aberrê. According to Cruz, Aberrê was a skillful capoeira practitioner: he was in fact Mestre Pastinha's best student in the CECA and a close friend of Mestre Bimba. Aberrê was so good that he even surpassed his *mestre* in skills (Cruz 2006: 165). He was known, however, for his violent character, and his aggression made him a very feared practitioner in the *rodas*. Bola Sete describes him: "Aberrê was a very smart *capoeirista* but due to any insignificant thing [that happened to him], he looked for revenge. It is said that one day he perceived a man in the music ensemble playing the tambourine wrong in a street *roda*. He reprimanded him, but not giving any importance to it, the man continued playing as if he were slapping the musical instrument. This was enough to make Aberrê use his pocketknife to cut the man's face before the other *capoeirista* could react" (Cruz 2006: 166).

This is just one of the stories concerning Aberrê's impatient and violent temper. His attitude and conduct were completely against the ethical precepts espoused by Mestre Pastinha. He was not the only capoeira practitioner who found it difficult to follow the teachings and philosophies of the mythical Mestre Pastinha.

Other *mestres* found it difficult to align the violent context of capoeira with the self-control and self-discipline imposed by Pastinha's academy. In time, and because of the institutionalization of the Angola style and the diminishing influence of street capoeira, violence began to appear in *rodas* in a disguised fashion. According to Oliveira Cruz, that violence was controlled and contained by the 1970s, but not suppressed completely. Conflicts between *mestres* were solved in the *roda* by means of performance. As deception took more relevance in practice, trickery and cunning became the vehicles of expressing symbolic violence and power relations.

In the same book by Oliveira Cruz we find another interesting anecdote, this one describing the confrontation between Nego David and Bom Cabrito, two excellent capoeira practitioners in the 1970s who, inexplicably, had never met in a *roda* but who had heard constantly about one another. Oliveira Cruz mentions that David decided that he was not going to miss any more *rodas* in order to find Bom Cabrito and play with him, once and for all:

> Finally, after some weeks, when he [David] arrived at the *roda*, he was introduced to Bom Cabrito. After they had been introduced to each other, both remained in anticipation of seeing one or the other play in order to know their game [strategies]. However, neither of them took the initiative [to play in the *roda*]. When a *capoeirista* called David to play, he refused, and Bom Cabrito did the same. Mestre Waldemar, observing the trickery of both players, decided to call a song insinuating that the *roda* was coming to an end. ... Not wanting to be left out of participating in the *roda*, Bom Cabrito decided to take the initiative and called David to play, which he accepted promptly. The game, after a short time, became more and more difficult; both players felt the great capacity of the other, until Bom Cabrito succeeded to break into the guard of David by kicking him fully in the face. Although the kick had been controlled not to cause more harm ... fearing the worst consequences, the mestre [Waldemar] called both players to the foot of the *Berimbau* with a special rhythm and ended the game. (Cruz 2006: 180)

The victory of Bom Cabrito shows the complex tension that exists between shrewdness, cunning, and open violence. In this episode, Cruz mentions that Mestre Waldemar praised the quality of the bout in order to criticize the following one executed by two of his students who had just performed acrobatic moves without any hint of cunning. He said that the encounter between Bom Cabrito and David was a real capoeira performance but the second one was just a circus act. He said that a genuine capoeira bout needed to include trickery, malice, and cunning together with a latent possibility of violence. Playing using exclusively acrobatic movements without a deceptive dialogue between the adversaries was an empty act used for tourists and exhibitions (Cruz 2006: 180–81).

Mestre Waldemar believed that cunning and trickery were the strategies that made capoeira Angola valuable and interesting. Years before Mestre Bola Sete described the scene quoted above, Pastinha had stressed that the element of malice was a core part of capoeira Angola. He opted for an ethical perspective in order to gain an understanding about how to control the aggressive side of the martial art and its consequences. Waldemar, on the other hand, believed that trickery and malice were the highest virtues or skills a practitioner could achieve.

Current *mestres* like Moraes and Cobra Mansa, for instance, define the attitudes of cunning and trickery more generally with the term *"malícia."* They say this concept is a mediator between violence and playfulness. In fact, Greg Downey says that the meaning of *malícia* is different from its English equivalent, malice. In Brazilian society, *malícia* has positive connotations. It is praise of someone who is clever and astute enough to achieve some goal independently of the means utilized. Downey prefers to use the term "cunning" as the closest translation of *malícia* (Downey 2005: 123). I agree with him in the sense that malice does not directly correlate as a translation for *malícia* and that cunning suits best for describing the skillful qualities of a capoeira practitioner.

Lowell Lewis, on the other hand, characterizes *malícia* as a mediated state between fight and dance (Lewis 1995: 231) that could be paired together with cunning and deception, since *malícia* embodies the art of being crafty, deceptive, and dexterous. However, in capoeira Angola *"malícia"* is not the only term that is used to praise the abilities of a player. As I mentioned above, *manha* and *malandragem* were the two concepts most commonly used during my research, when *mestres* and students alike characterized the skills of a capoeira practitioner. The use of English terms like "trickery," "deception," "malice," "roguery," or "cunning" could be suitable translations of these Portuguese terms, but they do not do full justice to the true meanings of these words. Instead of taking for granted a literal translation and its implicit meaning, I prefer to remain at the local level of interpretation and use *manha, malandragem,* and *malícia* in order to define *mestres'* perspectives on the playful and violent sides of capoeira.

Malícia and *manha* are used sometimes indistinctly to refer to the characteristics of a bout. In the two examples described by Oliveira, Waldemar said that the first interaction was based on the foundations of *malícia,* but the second one was not. The first one encompassed suitable attitudes and the ideals of capoeira Angola as a deceptive practice; the second one he described as a circus-like spectacle. *Malícia,* in this sense, is paired with cunning.

When Mestre Waldemar makes the distinction between a "real" game and a "circus" performance, he is describing opposite situations in which *malícia* is either present or absent. I found that *mestres* recognized that some bouts in capoeira Angola are extremely boring, containing long tedious sequences of the same types of moves with no *malícia*. For these types of *jogos* they have a name: *jogos de feijão com arroz* (games of rice and beans, which is the staple food of Bahian cuisine). According to some *mestres*, an interaction without *malícia* between two practitioners is like rice and beans: good, but too predictable, and without depth.

There is a second type of game that lacks the basic elements of *malícia* and *manha*, called *jogo de compadres* (game of comrades). According to my informants, capoeira practitioners are frequently caught in this type of game. It is a game played by friends who do not want to show violent behavior and whose intentions could be interpreted as signs of respect between them; the game is used as a way to greet an old friend. A *jogo de compadres* often lacks the elements of trickery and cunning found in other confrontations, and looks more like an exhibition where players experiment with acrobatic moves without regard for whether they are leaving themselves vulnerable. Sometimes a game starts as a *jogo de compadres* because the players would like to analyze their opponents' moves and discern their hidden intentions. After a few minutes, the players may start risking more, speeding up their interactions, and increasing the intensity of the bout. The game sanctioned by Waldemar as being a circus performance would probably look much the same as a *jogo de compadres.*

Although the words "*malícia*" and "*manha*" are used interchangeably in some cases, *mestres* consider that there are distinctions between the two terms. Mestre Valmir, for instance, said that *manha* emphasizes different resources designed to defeat an adversary with clean moves. On the contrary, *malícia* would imply being *manhoso* (tricky), but also being more clever than your opponent. *Malícia* describes the use of underhanded skills and methods that are not considered ethically correct, that mislead an adversary by hiding one's intentions. Valmir pointed out that one could learn *manha* in the classroom and technically apply it in the game. *Malícia* would be more difficult to achieve because it has to do with your own personality and other aspects that cannot be taught in the same way as *manha*. *Malícia*, Valmir told me, is simply "something that comes with you, something that is in yourself." In this sense, it shares characteristics with the concept of *mandinga,* which is impossible to teach.

Malandragem

Malandragem (see chapter 4) is not a concept exclusively used in capoeira. It is part of Brazilian society in general. As Roberto DaMatta noted, the *malandro* (rogue), belongs to the realm of those excluded from society—those marginal characters whose liminal positions allows them to be a kind of antihero: "The rogue is a being out of place, dislocated from the formal rules that govern the social structure, relatively excluded from the labor market—indeed, we define and represent him as one totally averse to work and highly individualized in his typical way of walking, his seductive mode of speaking, and in his singular dressing" (DaMatta 1991: 209).

DaMatta mentions that the *malandro* possesses a dual ethical foundation that fluctuates between moral and immoral respectability. He is an ambiguous character that acts at the same time as a respected, charismatic person and as a dishonest, underhanded, lawless being. He is a kind of trickster. It is by being placed in this liminal position that the *malandro* obtains his power.

Capoeira *mestres* and academic researchers alike identify the dual ethics of the *malandro* as something that is constitutive of capoeira Angola practitioners. According to Greg Downey, "*Malícia* guides both the *malandro* and the *Capoeirista*.... The texture of capoeira movement itself, like the virtuoso dribbling of Brazilian soccer stars, embodies *malandragem,* and allegedly cunning can be 'caught' from doing the art. One can become a rogue by doing capoeira" (Downey 2005: 119). Deception, then, creates *malandros* out of capoeira practitioners.

Many of these practitioners would agree with this characterization of their behavior. Lowell Lewis points out that, through *malandragem,* persons bend the rules and test the boundaries of practice and conventions without really breaking them (Lewis 1999: 547).

However, why is it necessary to be a *malandro* in capoeira? A tentative answer could be found in the two basic and apparently contradictory attitudes of playfulness and violence, which guide bodily interaction and permeate the lives of those who see capoeira as a way of life. In this sense, the concept of the *corpo fechado* discussed in chapter 3 is an expression of the conundrum between playfulness and violence. The emergence of the *corpo fechado* happens when practitioners face the ambiguity of a social practice that is indeterminate and difficult to classify.

The relationship between capoeira Angola and Candomblé provides a more general scope for an understanding of practice. It allows one to perceive the common attributes between these Afro-Brazilian traditions and their cosmological implications. The concept of *mandinga* is an example of the spiritual and mystical connotations that are embedded in capoeira and that define the way playfulness and violence are displayed.

Thus, *malandragem* appears as the perfect adaptive attitude toward the puzzle of capoeira, which is defined simultaneously as a martial art, a ritual, a game, and a dance. A *mestre* becomes a dual or even plural person, an individual embodying multiple layers within his being, using different sides of his personality according to the situations in which he is engaged and capable of manipulating the normative spheres in which he is immersed. It is not by chance that capoeira *mestres* refer to *malandragem* at the beginning of a *roda*. During the opening song, the chorus praises the *malandragem* of the participants (although there are no songs that specifically use *malandragem* as a central theme):

> Hey! God is great
> Hey! My *mestre* is great
> Hey! He taught me
> Hey! The roguery.[4]

The framework of the dual ethics of the *malandro* does not seem to create conflict among capoeira Angola practitioners. On the contrary, it is something that has positive connotations and is perceived frequently among players as something that confirms their status and the knowledge they are obtaining. The art of *malandragem* also puts capoeira practitioners on constant alert toward any possible act of treason by other practitioners. It is not by chance that *mestres* like Moraes often use the analogy of guerrilla warfare to characterize capoeira Angola. The *roda* is a place where practitioners need to be aware of unpredictable danger all the time (Downey 2005: 123).

If the *malandro* fluctuates between a blurred sense of morality, then the capoeira practitioner enacts this dual fluctuation in the *roda*. The idea of being an underhanded, astute *malandro* makes a capoeira practitioner, particularly a *mestre,* an unreliable, dangerous character—someone whose unpredictability and deceptive behavior helps him exert his power over others. He is a trickster who plays and juggles with the norms and expands or restricts them according to his own interests.

In a sense, the capoeira player bears a resemblance in some of his attitudes to the figure of the clown studied by Don Handelman (1990). Handelman's clown is a character that forms part of a liminal, ambivalent categorization of culture: "The clown type is an ambivalent figure of enticement and danger, hilarity and gravity, fun and solemnity" (Handelman 1990: 236). A clown is part of the anti-structure of a ritual event, a negation of the formal structure. A clown is not only part of a comedy; his function goes beyond humor and laughing: "Its internal composition enables the type [clown] to dissolve paradigms, thereby to make uncertain the relationships among those parts ordered by such boundaries. So, the type breaks down context and 'shakes up' reality on a number of levels, from the cosmic to the visceral" (Handelman 1990: 263).

The in-between of the clown is the in-between of the capoeira practitioner, too. The conundrum of the dual ethics expressed by playfulness and violence, together with the deceptive embodiment of a practice that refuses classification, exacerbate the symbolic tensions that capoeira practitioners, particularly *mestres*, face throughout their lives. Some *mestres* attribute the ambiguity of capoeira Angola to the world; it is constitutive of its cosmology. *Malícia, manha,* and *malandragem* cannot be fully taught in the classroom; like *mandinga,* these three notions refer to attitudes one learns through life, by being in the world.

Mestres affirm that practitioners of capoeira Angola abroad need to come to Salvador at least once in their lifetime in order to experience capoeira Angola "for real." This "for real" means to get involved in the daily life of deception, roguery, and trickery lived in the city, beyond the doors of the academies. It is in this environment that one can fully understand the meaning of playful violence and the invention of embodied solutions to an apparently irresolvable conundrum.

Redefining Playfulness

The in-between characterization of capoeira Angola and its ambiguous ethics makes of playfulness a key concept that permeates the logic of practice and its cosmological and powerful connotations. *Mestres* are the masters of deception and experts in performing acts of cunning. Therefore, it is important to describe the cultural connotations of playfulness from a local perspective and to redefine what capoeira practitioners think about play in general.

In the first place, there is a precision that needs to be addressed concerning the literal translation from Portuguese into English about the concept of play. As Floyd Merrel (2005: 44) has pointed out, in English there is a distinction between play and game that is absent in Portuguese and other Latin-derived languages. In Portuguese, the verb *jogar* and the noun *jogo* encompass altogether the notions of play and game. To play musical instruments, one uses the verb *tocar* (literally to touch). These slight differences, which could appear as superfluous, are important elements in any analysis of the relationship between playfulness and structural social norms. For capoeira practitioners, *jogar* encompasses not only the act of free engagement (play), but also the contextual framework of structures and rules (game).

The anthropology and sociology dedicated to the study of play has a tendency to give an idealized perception of playing. For instance, French sociologist Jean Duvignaud (1979, 1982) opposes play constantly to the seriousness of productive work. He locates the act of playing as the basic response that distinguishes human beings from animals and condemns the institutional world for ignoring the importance of play as an intrinsic human faculty. He says that institutional thought leaves aside "the part of utopia, randomness, and uncertainty, without which human life would not be different from those of ants or bees" (Duvignaud 1982: 15). For him, the act of playing is related to the ephemeral or the short-lived, to acts of experience that lack any social function and finality in the social system. To play, in this sense, is "an act without concept, aesthetic in principles and having a tendency to a universal and unreachable fraternity" (ibid.: 67). Play is thus opposed to current social and structural norms and implies a complete separation from imperative conducts; it is creative and free. It would form part of an anti-structural or a-structural force against the social constraint of culture.

The form of play found in capoeira Angola is not simply associated with free expression and anti-structural impulses. Playfulness is indissolubly linked to a fighting side, to latent violence, dangerousness, and seriousness. Therefore, capoeira Angola cannot be utterly understood as pure play if the concept of play is defined as complete freedom. Because it has to deal with a deadly seriousness, an aggressive side, through the implementation of a series of implicit rules, capoeira Angola encompasses playfulness within a very disruptive normative world. In this respect, Victor Turner's idea of play implying seriousness, including aspects of the structural world, is preferable. In Turner's view, play is presented as an elusive category that permeates the social structures; it is an imminent liminal and liminoid mode in the betwixt and between of culture (Turner 1982, 1986). Turner says, "Play is neither ritual action nor meditation, nor is it merely vegetative, nor is it just 'having fun'; it also has a good deal of ergotropic and agonistic aggressivity in its odd-jobbing, *bricolage* [emphasis in original] style" (Turner 1986: 31).

The relationship between play and seriousness has also been highlighted by Gregory Bateson in his book, *Steps to an Ecology of Mind:* "Play is a phenomenon in which the actions of 'play' are related to, or denote, other actions of 'not play.' We therefore meet in play with an instance of signals standing for other events, and it appears, therefore, that the evolution of play may have been an important step in the evolution of communication" (Bateson 1987: 187).

For Bateson, "play" means a form of communication that evokes instances not only determined by the rules of the game but also constitutes a meta-language that says something about the social world. He considers some elements to be part of a map-territory relation, a logical construction that creates coordinates between the contents of a message. In capoeira, latent violence is the eruption of "deadly seriousness." It is the potency of threat and deceit.

The relationship between playfulness and violence constitutive of capoeira makes the boundaries between play and seriousness difficult to discern. Although practitioners call capoeira a game and refer to its practice as *brincar* (free play without restrictions), the nature of the contextual frame is labile (Bateson 1987: 189). It is not possible to affirm with certainty where the connotations of play end and when violence arises. This is part of the paradoxical situation of capoeira, a paradox that emerges from the apparently untrue or unmeant character of the messages exchanged by playful interaction and the nonexistence of what is being denoted by deceptive, violent practice (ibid.: 190). In a sense, the paradox is even deeper than Bateson frames it to be. For Bateson, the paradox is attenuated when the players recognize the untrue character of play as its explanatory principle. Due to the intricacies of playfulness and violence in capoeira, however, it is not possible to define the untruthful character of playful action so easily. Capoeira elements are true and play is a matter of seriousness, prestige, status, and—above all—power.

There is tension between the norms inherent to the practice of capoeira Angola and the structure of Brazilian society in Salvador. This is a tension that playfulness and violence exacerbate. This gives rise to the intensity of emotions and passions that constitute the subjective experience of practitioners when they face ambiguous normative boundaries or, as Victor Turner believed, when they are immersed in liminal experiences. On some occasions, *mestres* embody the norms; on others, they are subject to the dictates of the CAC and the lineages of knowledge. The difficulty to discern boundaries is produced by the tension that exist between playfulness and violence. Don Handelman has described how the paradoxical discernment of boundaries operates: "A boundary may be seen as composed of contradictory sets of attributes: top/bottom, known/strange, inclusion/exclusion, and so on. Paradoxically, if a boundary is of the inside, then it also is of the outside like a moebius strip. These contraries are not resolved, in and of themselves: instead their figure–ground relationship continuously shifts. If the internal constitution of a boundary is paradoxical, then the paradox (and therefore the boundary) is self-referential, closed, and impenetrable" (Handelman 1990: 247).

In capoeira Angola, this paradox entails a mutual implication between playfulness and violence. For example, a bout in a *roda* could become more and more aggressive until the audience believes that violence may erupt at any time (and, subsequently, a fight). The two practitioners might control their emotions and disguise their anger by laughing and using acrobatic moves. The bout may continue to enact the language of playfulness, although the tension between play and violence is latent all the time.

A clear boundary may transform a bout of capoeira Angola into a quarrel: the open use of physical and verbal violence. These break the limits of play and players recognize it very clearly. Although capoeira Angola sanctions the use of blows, if practitioners use their hands it is always as a way of protecting their bodies, to stop *cabeçadas*, or to distract an opponent. In a *roda*, if someone loses his temper and resorts to blows (hitting an opponent with a fist), then the playfulness of capoeira dissipates and an open fight could start. In these rare but documented occasions, a *roda* transforms into a battlefield. However, during my time in the city of Salvador I never saw a bout in a *roda* transformed thus into an open brawl. My friends and informants told me that maybe only in festivals and street *rodas* you could see fights, but never inside an academy. The boundaries between playfulness and violence are always tested but ultimately are controlled by the *mestres* in such cases.

Mestre Canjiquina wrote, "Capoeira is a game of double meaning. It has two faces rarely separable" (Silva 1989: 2). I believe he meant these two faces to be the fighting and artistic sides of capoeira, encompassed within an ambiguous ethical framework dictated by deception and cunning. If violence is controlled, it is because it still lingers in the capoeira *roda* in the form of an always available possibility. It is this potential that makes violence more dangerous, because it is an apprehension of its uncertainty and unpredictability. It does not matter if the danger rarely erupts—the importance is that people can feel it in their bones, that it reminds us that violence is always a possibility.

Deeper than Deep Play

As a last remark concerning playfulness and violence in capoeira, I would like to return to the classic analysis made by Clifford Geertz on the Balinese cockfight (Geertz 2000) and his concept of deep play, where social and psychological issues are at stake in the secluded realm of betting. Betting, Geertz argues, is not about money but about status; it forms part of a differential hierarchy between "status gambling" and "money gambling" (Geertz 2000: 435).

A cockfight mirrors and dramatizes culture. According to Geertz, play does not change people's status in Balinese society, nor does it endanger the integrity of the players. It simply structures the general human themes of "death, masculinity, rage, pride, loss, benefice, chance" (Geertz 2000: 445). One might say the same of capoeira Angola. In a *roda*, playfulness reflects the hierarchy and power of the *mestres*. This is displayed through their bodily movements, dexterity, skills, and music. *Mestres, contramestres, treinels*, advanced students, and beginners all become recognized through practice. *Mestres* in particular can seduce an audience. They can wrap their acts with a powerful, mystical aura that intimidates and controls their adversaries; they can show their magical power and their *mandinga* while playing or singing.

Capoeira Angola, however, is more than just a practice mirroring or dramatizing the whole of Bahian society. In a structural sense, there is an inversion of hierarchical roles and a real transformation of status. In capoeira the hierarchy is controlled by powerful members of Afro-Brazilian culture, who in other social circumstances would find themselves excluded or relegated from important positions of power. They order and rule their academies in a vertical distribution of power over middle-class Bahians and foreigners. However, capoeira Angola's significance is more than just the expression of status in an oppressed race. It displays Afro-Brazilian values in opposition to those of middle-class and elite Bahians. It is a cultural practice of resistance.

Therefore, playfulness in capoeira does not mirror a hierarchical structure; it inverts the structure. Contrary to the Balinese cockfight, where nothing important is at stake, capoeira Angola is a practice that really can change the economical and sociocultural status of the persons who ascend in the hierarchy of power, especially those who possess titles such as *contramestre* and *mestre*. Practicing capoeira Angola produces palpable effects.

Practitioners also consider capoeira a ritual, with real consequences at stake; they may get injured or humiliated through subtle acts of violence. Power is built on an ongoing process of apprenticeship and accumulation of experience, which is absent in the deep play analyzed by Geertz. For him, the cockfight merely represents a drama but lacks social agency. For him, it is "an image, fiction, a model, a metaphor, the cockfight is a means of expression; its function is neither to assuage social passions nor to heighten them (although, in its playing-with-fire way it does a bit of both) but, in a medium of feathers, blood, crowds, and money, to display them" (Geertz 2000: 444).

Following the cockfight, individuals return to their normal lives unchanged and things continue as if nothing had happened. The only sufferers are the cocks (Geertz 2000: 443); the status and integrity of the players remain the same. There is nothing more distant from the reality of capoeira, where play is felt in the flesh and where practice also involves defiance. In some cases, serious cosmic battles may occur between powerful subjects who manipulate imperceptibly and deceptively mystical forces. Therefore, the modality of playfulness displayed in capoeira Angola is more than simple play; it is a matter of seriousness. In sum, it is a total social fact that does not merely represent, but that in fact presents life in its full intensity.

Notes

1. For the sake of argument, I use the words "moral" or "morality" and "ethics" as synonyms, although I am aware of their philosophical and conceptual differences.
2. It is important to mention that there are constant efforts in the *roda* to avoid gender distinctions. Men and women alike (in theory) must follow the same dictates of deception, playfulness, and symbolic violence. Although this is fomented in academies, in the reality of capoeira Angola circles gender matters (Joseph 2005). Ascension in the hierarchy of knowledge is an almost exclusive prerogative of male practitioners. Although changes con-

cerning the role played by women in academies has improved, there are still substantial obstacles preventing female practitioners from achieving the same status and recognition as their male counterparts.

3. Pastinha published during his lifetime a small book called *Capoeira Angola*. However, after his death, his friend Carybé made public a series of unpublished manuscripts written by the mythical *mestre*. In these manuscripts (which are, by the way, very difficult to read and to systematize), Pastinha delved into the mysteries of capoeira Angola. In an effort to make these statements coherent, Angelo Decanio published the book *Heritage of Mestre Pastinha*, a work that follows Pastinha's ideas together with commentaries made by Decanio. The notes cited in this section of the chapter come from Decanio's publication.

4. Iê! viva meu deus
   Iê! viva meu mestre
   Iê! que me ensinou
   Iê! A malandragem.

CHAPTER 6

♫ How Musical Instruments Become Persons
The Power of Materiality

An ethnographic description of capoeira Angola must include the music. In a *roda,* music creates a playful and artistic atmosphere, which gives to capoeira a special ritual and spiritual aura. Capoeira music connects with the themes of power, cosmology, and practice discussed in previous chapters. Musical instruments play a role in the development of a particular ontology that blurs the boundaries between subjects and objects. Therefore, this last chapter is concerned with materiality[1] and its aesthetic effects. I argue that certain objects in capoeira have the potential to become persons, and that the aesthetic effects of materiality give *mestres* conclusive evidence about their power in practice. It also justifies the existence of a pyramidal hierarchical structure.

The aesthetic effects that musical instruments possess fuse together persons with materials and sounds. Objects have agency (Gell 1998) and affect social relations—sometimes in unimaginable ways. Sociologists and anthropologists alike have highlighted the complex social existence of objects (see Appadurai 1986; Bataille 1991; Baudrillard 1997; Henare et al. 2007; Latour 1993, 2002, 2005; Mauss 2002; Miller 1987, 2005; Sahlins 1976; Strathern 1999; Wagner 1986a), particularly concerning how simple materials become other things depending on the contexts in which they appear, the reasons for their being exchanged or used, and their role as mediators or creators of relations. All of these authors coincide in the power that objects have in creating relations and ties among humans.

In this chapter, I focus exclusively on the importance that the *berimbau* acts in the *rodas* as an agent of personification. The discussion offers an argument that centers on the power of agency and sound. I argue that music provides an example of the acoustic agency of materials, which makes evident a *mestre's* source of power in practice. Music, in other words, is another channel through which magical power flows.

The African Origins of the *Berimbau*

The *berimbau* began to be viewed as the symbol of capoeira fairly recently. This recognition is a phenomenon that probably accompanied the process of institutionalization and codification of styles in academies. The origins of the *berimbau*, however, are uncertain, and its history is still unclear. The instrument does not appear in connection with capoeira in paintings, official documents, newspapers, or police records in Salvador until approximately 1930. Before this period, little is known about its presence in Afro-Brazilian capoeira (Abreu 1999; Assunção 2005; Dias 2006; Oliveira 2005). Rio de Janeiro also lacks testimonies of the existence of the *berimbau* among capoeira practitioners in the nineteenth century (Soares 2001). Thus, the literature on capoeira has yet to determine what moment and in what circumstances the *berimbau* became part of the practice.

What we know so far is that the history of the *berimbau* dates to the early nineteenth century. Peter Fryer, in a book that traces the relationship between Brazilian and African music, describes how an instrument resembling a *berimbau* captured the attention of foreigners in different regions of Brazil (Fryer 2000). Fryer points to Henry Koster, the son of a sugarcane plantation owner in the region of Ceará, who characterizes an instrument resembling the *berimbau* in his book *Travels to Brazil:* "He described it as 'a large bow with one string, having half of a coco-nut shell or of a small gourd strung upon it. This is placed against the abdomen, and the string is struck with the finger, or with a small bit of wood'" (Koster quoted in Fryer 2000: 35). Although Koster does not provide the social context in which the string instrument appears, it is one of the earliest descriptions available of the *berimbau.*

Fryer mentions that one of the most important visual registers of an instrument resembling a *berimbau* is found in the French artist Jean Baptiste Debret's portrait "The Old African Orpheus (Oricongo)". Debret lived in Brazil from 1816 to 1831 (Fryer 2000: 35). The music bow depicted in the portrait does not appear related to capoeira or to any public ritual, however. The fact that it is referred to by other names, like the above-mentioned *oricongo* or *urucungo*, indicates that the name *berimbau* might not have been widely used in this period.

In his comparative analysis, Fryer concludes that the origins of the music bow reside in Africa, in the region of Angola: "Just as the elements of capoeira are clearly of African origin, so the berimbau, though it has evolved to its present form in Brazil, clearly derives from various Angolan gourd-resonated single-string musical bows played with a thin cane stick. It has several notable precursors" (Fryer 2000: 32). He cites ethnologist Gerhard Kubik, who highlighted the similarities between the music bows used in Angola and in Brazil. Fryer mentions that Kubik was convinced that the similarities extended also to how the music bow was played on both sides of the Atlantic and the similarity in structure (Fryer 2000: 33). Historian Matthias Assunção also agrees with the African origin of the *berimbau* and the *caxixi:* "The Brazilian *berimbau* derives from Central African music bows, but the woven rattle [*caxixi*] that accompanies it in Brazil is likely to be of West African origin" (Assunção 2005: 40). Key Shaffer also mentions that instruments similar in structure and sound to the *berimbau* exist in many different places along the African West Coast (Shaffer 1977). For ethnomusicologist Richard Graham, the origins of the *berimbau* are strongly associated with the Hungu people of Luanda and the Mbulumbumba ethnic group in Southeast Angola (Graham 1991: 2).

The comparative evidence at hand seems to offer a strong argument in favor of the African origins of the *berimbau* (see also Brito 2012). I do not deny the likelihood that the instrument originated in Africa, but one must be careful when using a comparative theoretical framework that has as one of its premises exclusively the search for origins. Assunção warns us that the theories of survivals and purity found in Afrocentric discourses could provide a distorted view of cultural practices (Assunção 2005: 20–22). Although he considers the positive sides of moving away from Eurocentric paradigms in historical and cultural analysis of the African diaspora (ibid.: 24), he is against radical Afrocentric ideological approaches that have tried to prove, sometimes without conclusive evidence, the extension of African cultural traits in different parts of the world. Assunção is concerned with the manipulation of historical facts that Afrocentric scholars incur when writing about the possibility of African continuities in capoeira. He says, "The anxiety to prove African continuities or capoeira's Angolan origins, however, ended up inducing a number of scholars to neglect some elementary rules of academic research, such as the respect for the statements made by the original sources. For some, Kongo/Angola has now become the mythical home of all martial arts of the diaspora, to the point that these writers should be qualified Kongo—rather than Afrocentric" (ibid. 2005: 25).

The risk of resurrecting a long defunct diffusionist model of cultural explanation should be avoided. In the analysis of materiality, one must be aware that cultural objects form part of a local context that shapes them and gives them meaning. In the case of capoeira, the important question is not to prove that the *berimbau* is of African origin. The central matter is to know how this instrument is locally meaningful, how it became an essential part of capoeira, what *mestres* say about its African origins, and the stories *mestres* tell about the instrument. Thus, the perspective of the *mestres* will provide the necessary lens through which we may analyze the meaning of the music bow.

The *Berimbau* and the Practice of Capoeira

As I have described above, capoeira Angola differs from other capoeira styles in the importance given to music. While music exists in the performances and is part of the *rodas* of other styles, the connotations of music are different in capoeira Angola because they relate intrinsically to a particular cosmology and to an exclusive form of viewing power.

Capoeira Angola music allows little rhythmic variation and experimentation, either with the instruments or within songs. Capoeira music has standard rhythms and there is no room for much variation. Improvisation is performed mainly by *berimbaus,* while the other instruments have the obligation to keep a steady beat. As Greg Downey mentions, a steady repetitive rhythm may function to affect the bodies of participants: "Instrumental rhythms affect how the game unfolds, control the severity of competition, and set the style of interaction. ... Unlike singing, instrumental music influences play constantly, interacting at every moment with the way the players move" (Downey 2005: 87). Because the three *berimbaus* are considered the most important instruments in the ensemble, they have the obligation to guide the music and actions of participants.

Mestres of capoeira Angola consider the *berimbau* to be an essentially African instrument that builds a direct connection with their ancestors. Many *mestres* have pursued the search for their African roots by traveling to different parts of the African continent (for instance, Angola), including the coast of Benin, Mozambique, and Nigeria. In their quest, these *mestres* have seen musical instruments similar to the *berimbau.*

I propose that these firsthand experiences have helped leaders to reaffirm their conviction about the African continuities of the *berimbau* and its importance in every academy of capoeira Angola in Brazil.

Perhaps influenced by the works of historians, leaders of capoeira affirm that the *berimbau* did not have a musical purpose in Brazil. In the beginning, it was used as a bell by rubbish collectors to attract the attention of people in the central neighborhoods of Salvador. This is the standard story explaining the origins of the *berimbau,* and I registered at least six or seven different variations of the same narrative.

Mestres commented that capoeira was an urban phenomenon, and so persons linked to criminal activities, disorder, and vagrancy played it in the streets. These persons, together with practitioners who worked in the ports as stevedores, marines, and carriers, were responsible for the introduction of the *berimbau* in public performances (Dias 2006).

According to the late Frederico de Abreu, one of the most renowned specialists in capoeira studies, capoeira players in the beginning of the twentieth century used *atabaques* as their main musical instruments. He said that practitioners played the *atabaques* in the same way they did in the Afro-Brazilian religion of Candomblé. Abreu indicates that *berimbaus* supplanted drums in public performances for two reasons: portability and convenience. Because capoeira was played in the streets, portability was extremely important. *Berimbaus* were more practical to move from one place to another than *atabaques,* which are heavy instruments. Abreu told me that capoeira practitioners perhaps adapted the use of *berimbaus* to imitate the rhythmic patterns used by drums. He commented that this transition must have happened smoothly and almost spontaneously.

From the 1940s onward, documentation indicates that the *berimbau* became essential for the practice of all capoeira styles; the instrument could be seen in almost every capoeira performance in the street, and in photographs from the time (Downey 2005).

The Personification of the *Berimbau*

The *berimbau* is the central musical instrument in the *rodas.* Consequently, this has brought an increasing specialization of its music potential (Downey 2002). This is evident, for instance, in the creative complexity of tunes, rhythms, and melodies that mark the *berimbau's* innovative performances. To learn how to play the *berimbau* is a requirement in any academy and is part of the *mestres'* daily teachings, to such an extent that leaders consider a player who does not wish to learn how to play a *berimbau,* a lame player, or a *capenga,* meaning a fake and incomplete person (Downey 2005: 88).

The sacredness surrounding the *berimbau* transforms an exclusive material perception of the object into an intrinsic subjective experience (subjective in the sense of developing social attributes, just like a subject). The first step to this subjective transformation is the fabrication of the instrument. Although nowadays members of the academies buy sticks to make the *berimbaus* in local markets or purchase them through intermediaries (Brito 2012), twenty or thirty years ago it was still common for players to go into the *mato* (forest) in the interior of the Bahian province to cut the *beribas* directly, according to Mestre Decanio. He thinks that there are still persons who go into the forest, despite the growing commercialization and availability of ready-cut sticks. Decanio emphasizes that the commercial trade of *beribas* has not undermined the tradition of making your own *berimbau.*

Mestre Boca do Rio agrees with Decanio. He explained that there was a special relationship that a player created with his *berimbau* during the process of fabrication.[2] For him, the fabrication of his own *berimbau* created an intimate and inseparable connection between him and the instrument. By forcing students to build their own instruments from scratch, Boca facilitated an experiential way of getting closer to the sacredness of the musical instrument. Boca said that, as time goes by, one begins to treat the *berimbau* like a friend, a confidant, and a protector. A *berimbau* might last between three to ten years, and in some cases even longer. Players thus spend a substantial amount of time with the instrument and create an emotive relationship with it. In some cases, the *berimbau* becomes either an extension of the player or transforms itself into a new "teacher" (Downey 2002: 499).

However, it is in practice that the *berimbau* activates—that is, truly transforms into a person. As I have mentioned before, there is no *roda* without live music. Music creates a ritual atmosphere that is intensely experienced by practitioners. *Mestres* say that players understand how to perform the physical moves correctly through their interaction with the music; in sum, capoeira music orientates the bodily interactions of practitioners.

Therefore, the value of the *berimbau* as an essential instrument for capoeira has to do with bodily action and musical execution. The three *berimbaus* that form the core of the orchestra interact one with another; they also send messages to the two practitioners playing in the *roda*. According to Mestre Valmir, "*Berimbaus* speak to you, and they also speak to themselves." This is not just an embellished metaphor. *Berimbaus* actually sound (even for the noninitiated) as if they were speaking. They calibrate the intensity of performance with their hollow, strong sound, which penetrates the bodies of participants.

The *berimbau gunga* is known for being the leading voice of the orchestra (see Figure 6.1). The *berimbau medio* plays a *gunga* inverted tune, which brings out a steady dissonant melody. The *berimbau viola* plays like the *gunga,* but with a louder and sharp tune. The *gunga* and the *viola* are the most difficult *berimbaus* to master, and advanced students or *mestres* are the ones who play them in the *rodas*. The *viola* in particular is responsible for pitch variation and improvisation; it creates dissonance and breaks the melody (much like the lead guitar in rock or heavy metal music). *Mestres* say that the sound of the *viola* cuts through the sound of the other two *berimbaus* and creates new musical patterns based exclusively on improvisation.

Figure 6.1. Capoeira orchestra. From left to right: Mestre Boca do Rio, Mestre Poloca, and Mestra Paulinha. Photograph: Sergio González Varela. Date: 18 August 2006.

Mestres state that the three *berimbaus* generate such an intense effect in the *roda* that they transform themselves into subjects, or persons.
The *viola,* for instance, guides players to make unpredictable moves by
calling them. The dissonance inspires the moment for an attack or a
defense (see Figure 6.2). "It feels as if the *viola* is telling me what to do,
when to attack, when to defend myself," said Mestre Boca do Rio. *Berimbaus* also send warnings to the players who are interacting in the *roda.*
There are moments when these messages become more obvious, such
as when a *berimbau* string breaks during a *roda.* A *mestre* may interpret
this musical interruption as a warning to avoid playing with certain opponents. In other cases, the same interruption may be interpreted as a
sign of power activated by a superior player who breaks the string with
his spiritual force. While the break might be just the result of a rusty
string that could not hold any longer, *mestres* never allow the breaking
of a string to pass unnoticed; they will always try to find a reason that
goes beyond the realm of the proper material conditions of the string.

There is an intimate relationship between the acoustic sounds of
the *berimbaus* and the bodies of performers (Downey 2002). The acous-

Figure 6.2. Capoeira Music Orchestra at FICA–Bahia Salvador, Brazil.
Photograph: Sergio González Varela. Date: 4 October 2006.

tic experience activates bodily impulses and, through rhythmic, spontaneous dissonance, sounds send codified messages to players. These bits of information and meaning are embodied and made intelligible by players, just like words in speech.

Therefore, the sound and melody of the *berimbaus* form their own language, which is how they communicate to each other and to other people. Of course, this communication is incited by the person who is playing the instrument and his level in the hierarchy of knowledge. The sounds of the *berimbaus* are produced by the musician's intention and his fusion with the instrument, although the quality of the sound will vary depending on who is playing it. Agency thus occurs in a recursive way only when the *mestres* or other persons at the top level of the hierarchy play the instrument. Although any player can activate the sound of the *berimbau* by playing the instrument, only a person with power will be able to activate recursively the agency of the *berimbau*. In these cases, the *berimbau* becomes autonomous and independent; it takes control of the musician. Thus, while the *berimbau* condenses all the symbolic connotations related to capoeira's ancestry, mythical past, and tradition, there is an energetic or spiritual flow embodied by the instrument that makes it a subject, or a person. The enhanced energy condensed in the instrument affects the atmosphere of the *roda;* *mestres* argue that people can feel when a *berimbau* has power or becomes a person. On such occasions, a *berimbau* sounds louder and feels heavier than usual for the person who is playing it; he may experience that he hasn't enough energy to hold it for too long and must exchange it for another *berimbau,* or pass it to a leader because holding the instrument causes a lot of pain (see Figure 6.3). Such physical pain is one of the proofs that *mestres* give about the sacred and personified character of the *berimbau.*

Thus, a *mestre* and the instrument become inseparable. Initially, the *berimbau* is an extension of the player. Later, the player may become a medium for the spiritual autonomy of the instrument. This relationship illustrates what Wagner calls the simultaneous capacity of symbols both to stand for themselves and to be part of collective conventions. The analytical distance that separates symbols and references produces an artificial divide in-between that does not exist in practice. In action, both capacities and recursive moments between symbols and references are simply transitional and unconscious—they are moments of obviation (Wagner 1981: 35–70).

Berimbaus embody the qualities of a *mestre's* power. For these individuals, the instruments become alive in a certain way. The flow of the

Figure 6.3. *Roda* of capoeira at ACANNE. Extreme left, standing, Mestre Renê; with the instruments left to right, Mestre Boca Rica, Mestre Bigodinho, and Treinel Roque playing the *berimbaus;* standing in the back Mestres Lua Rasta and Iván. Photograph: Sergio González Varela. Date: 18 March 2006.

past in the present makes apparent the African ancestry of the instrument in the actuality of live performances. Leaders of capoeira make ancestral connections through music, and the *berimbau* brings the spirit of the mythical past to the present. But, as in the cases of mediums or in spirit possession, only those who have power and knowledge can establish such communication with the spirits. In a sense, making a *berimbau* speak is another way of showing power.

The personification of the *berimbau* brings a momentary glimpse of an ontology of music that transforms objects into persons—agents that affect social relations and the experience of participants. The ontology of music shows that materiality has an open-ended mutability. The process starts with the building of the instruments from scratch and extends to the familiarity that a practitioner obtains from an intimate connection with the musical possibilities of the instrument. It ends with the transformation of the *berimbau* into a sacred quasi-object, an autonomous person who communicates and channels the musician's *man-*

dinga. And yet there is still the role that aesthetic appreciation plays in the personification of the *berimbau.* I describe in the following section how the *berimbau* makes possible a particular aesthetic experience and a sublimation of the potentiality of power in practice.

The Aesthetics of Personification

The personification of the *berimbau* creates its own autonomy that shifts from an arbitrary symbolization that separates form and content to the amalgamation of both in one single form. Personification implies the conjunction of collective conventions and individual inventions. This is not only an ontological or epistemological characterization of a cultural practice, but also an aesthetic and subjunctive sublimation of experience.

Studies on materiality tend to query what kind of relations materiality creates (Strathern 1999). The problems posed by materiality are often perceived as mechanisms of consumption or moments for anthropological reflection. They are not easy to solve. While some recent discussions on the topic showed the autonomous force of materiality, it is necessary to know its agentive and pragmatic nature, too (Holbraad 2011). The pair of concepts—materiality and person—cannot be dissociated: their link is the initial step from which either autonomy or dependency occur.

In the West, different approaches to the understanding of objects in the world have made the mistake of trying to depurate things from any external input in the creation of meaning. Analyses invoking the death of the author, the autonomy of the system, and the self-contention of objects all reflect a further move of Western cosmology into acts of purification that condition the ontology of materiality (Latour 1993). This process seems to create an artificial meaning of materiality that conceals its own process of invention, circulation, and reception in society. In the ethnographic case of capoeira Angola, there is an aesthetic appreciation of the *berimbau,* one that goes first from the extension of the person toward the instrument and second from the independence of the instrument to its subsequent transformation into another person. Such autonomy is defined by sensuous qualities displayed by the object (in this case, the *berimbau*), such as acoustic hollowness, disharmony, interference, and dissonant improvised rhythms. If there is such a "thing-uese" or a language of things (Holbraad 2011: 10), the sensuous qualities are the way in which a particular thing communicates itself. In order to produce such a personified impact on the performers, the thing must appeal to an aesthetic appreciation of its qualities. It must activate into the listeners a proclivity to identify singular sounds and to receive them and act accordingly to their meaning. In a Wagnerian sense, we would say that the aesthetic experiences of individuals make possible their differentiation of a singular point within the flow of collective convention (Wagner 1981: 52). This singular point is the speaking of the thing, and is seen by practitioners as a moment of cultural invention.

Philosopher Hans-Georg Gadamer characterized the singularity of the aesthetic experience of an art object not only as a moment of invention but also as a moment of truth, which he defines as *cognitio sensitiva* a sensuous knowledge that possesses a quality of truth:

> In the realm of art above all, it is self-evident that the work of art is not experienced in its own right if it is only acknowledged as a link in a chain that leads elsewhere. The "truth" that is possessed for us does not consist in some universal regularity that merely presents itself through the work. Rather, *cognitio sensitiva* means that in the apparent particularity of sensuous experience (which we always attempt to relate to the universal), there is something in our experience of the beautiful that arrests us and compels us to dwell upon the individual appearance itself. (Gadamer 1986: 16)

The aesthetic experience produces a kind of knowledge that creates a moment of truth comparable to that of universal rationality. Its origins are not scientific, however—it comes from a fundamental human experience centered on the concepts of play, symbol, and festival. These three concepts make possible the development of relations that are not guided exclusively by an intentional, productive purpose. On the contrary, and like art, they establish a hermeneutic identity (Gadamer 1986: 25). Hermeneutic identity in Gadamerian terms is the key to understanding the truth of the work of art, since it requires the subject to play along in order to experience it: "The work issues a challenge that expects to be met. It requires an answer—an answer that can only be given by someone who accepted the challenge. And that answer must be his own, and given actively. The participant belongs to the play" (ibid.: 26).

To include the subject into the aesthetic experience of materiality is to construct a relationship that gives certainty to experience. This is why it is so easy for *mestres* of capoeira Angola to accept *berimbaus* as autonomous persons. As Gadamer points out, perception should mean something more than just a grasping of sounds and sensory impressions: "To perceive something is not to collect together utterly separate sensory impressions, but is rather ... to take something as true" (Gadamer 1986: 29). This "taking something as true" becomes, in Gadamer's terminology, an aesthetic of nondifferentiation. It encompasses the understanding of materiality as something truthful.

The aesthetic experience hinders any attempt at purifying materiality, as structural semiotics would argue. In fact, aesthetics binds persons and objects as relational moments in the search for truth. In the case of capoeira, it defines both the sacredness of the *berimbau* and the communion of participants in the *roda*. Through its music, the *berimbau* makes evident and intelligible[3] its message and its personifying quality. Aesthetics provides the transformation of the object, which is perceived initially as an instrument, into a person or agent. This is fulfilled by the acoustic melodies of the *berimbau* and the position of this instrument/person in the center of capoeira performances. In this case, we are not dealing with representation—rather, it is not a matter of belief or of local people getting things wrong. It is a matter of certainty and truth in a process of becoming and fusing. As capoeira *mestres* say, it is a moment of communion with what they deem to be their ancestral African roots, a communion that brings practitioners closer to the meaning of capoeira as an Afro-Brazilian art form. This is the truth they gain in the *rodas,* the truth that becomes evident in the listening of the *berimbau* in action.

The Transcendence of Materiality

The personification of materiality involves a differentiated ontology, which is based on a perspective that does not regard the relationship between materials and concepts as arbitrary. It is a movement of mutual implication that argues for the fusion of objects and subjects in a single recursive form. It is a "fusion of the worlds," as anthropologist Paul Stoller has argued (Stoller 1989, 31). It is part of a flow that becomes the basis for transformation and mutability.

The transformation of the *berimbau* into a person who speaks affects the bodies of leaders, guiding them in their movements in the *roda*. This agency is responsible for the intensity of the interaction. To activate this agency, a player with power uses an aesthetic mode of expression, which acts as an effective mechanism for revealing the *berimbau* as a person.

Gadamer's ideas contribute to an understanding of the personification of materiality as a moment of truth. In some way, this is what Greimas pursued in his later years, when he brought semiotics closer to the aesthetic apprehension of life as an ultimate truth and acknowledged the importance of the subject in the process of meaningful creation (Greimas 1997). I find that the dialectic and recursive strategy of personifying the *berimbau* speaks directly to Gell's idea about the agency of the art object and Marilyn Strathern's position on relatedness. Materials create relations, modify them, and even question their validity. It is a move that involves epistemological, ontological, and aesthetic qualities.

If possible, a new approach to materiality should move from a dialectical perspective between subject and object toward an aesthetic dimension, where our assumptions about materials must be cast into doubt in order to create, according to Martin Holbraad (2008a), new concepts or even new things to talk about and to talk with. This suspension of disbelief may elucidate the role that materiality plays in the formation of alterity and its anthropological, discursive presentation as an instance of the invention of culture.

Notes

1. The notion of "things," "objects," and "artifacts" should be understood here as heuristic terms. Although I am aware of conceptual and analytical differences in them within material culture studies, I use these terms indistinguishably in this chapter for discursive purposes.

2. The entire process consisted of cleaning the stick with sandpaper and a piece of a glass bottle, then cutting the gourds and making them suitable for the sticks. Following that, the steel wire was extracted from a car tire. A special ointment was added to cure (make resistant) the *beribas*. Then the rattle and playing stick were fabricated. The final step was the addition of leather protection at the top of the *beriba* and finding a good coin or stone to make the sound of the assembled *berimbau.*

3. In a different context and with different connotations, Martin Holbraad has stated the importance of evidence and truth as main topics of anthropological research (Holbraad 2008a). Although the case of Holbraad deals with the ethnographic context of Cuban divination and Ifá cults, there are parallelisms concerning the local apprehensions of what constitutes truth in capoeira.

ꝗ Epilogue

After a two-year break from training capoeira, I met my friend Boca do Rio again in August 2016. He was visiting Mexico City for a day. It had been six years since I'd seen him, and I did not want to miss the chance to see one of my most admired *mestres* while he was visiting my hometown. We met and talked briefly, because he was very busy teaching. We exchanged greetings and anecdotes. Boca told me that he has been traveling all over the world sharing his knowledge of capoeira, but that he is based in Bahia, after a long spell living in Santiago de Compostela, Spain. He could not stay far away from his roots, he said.

When the time came to say good-bye, Boca pulled me aside and told me not to give up capoeira, that the time to do something for the Angola community was now, and that he was confident that, at some point in my life, I would return to the *rodas*. He told me that, for the time being, at least, I could use the book I was writing as a form of continuing my commitment to capoeira, a way of sharing knowledge. It was a pity we did not have more time to talk, but when we said good-bye I promised him that next time we saw each other I would be back in training.

My journey following the capoeira *mestres* in their path of knowledge ends here, for the moment. I am still in touch with many of the *mestres,* however. The advent of social media has made possible to keep in touch with them more easily. Most capoeira leaders I know are avid Facebook users and post regularly. Through their videos, comments, and photos, I've been given a glimpse of their lives today. This does not provide the true depth of understanding that real interaction does, of course, but it complements all that I have learned during my research and in international workshops.

The *roda* of life is a circle, and in it you meet the people who are important when the time is right. I was fortunate to have met many capoeira *mestres* when I thought the time was right, and I continue to see how they impact other people's lives. I have had the pleasure to see other students and friends ascending in the hierarchy of knowledge, committed to their long path of apprenticeship. I have also seen many

others quit or stop practicing capoeira due to the unforeseen impon-
derables of life.

In general, long-term research in the field is difficult. It is a luxury
few researchers can afford today. I have been involved with capoeira for
more that sixteen years now, as a practitioner and as a researcher. I have
experienced many different sites and situations, and this has formed the
core of my writing in these pages. My aim was to offer a glimpse of the
importance of individual power in the construction of social practice.
Without my long-term involvement in capoeira, I would have never
been able to write a book like this. Dealing with *mestres* is not always
easy. Getting to know them is also difficult. Forging a close friendship
with some of them can be unthinkable. Like in Candomblé, in capoeira
one needs to be patient, receptive, and persistent, even when it seems
there is no reason to continue learning.

Within the pages of this book I hope to have offered a commensu-
rable description concerning a practice that is building a world in itself.
The ethnographic description of capoeira Angola in this book is by no
means exhaustive. Between the individual power and the hierarchies
and structures that capoeira creates, a whole world exists. Bodies move;
spirits and *orixás* are invoked; people play, seduce, attack, and deceive;
and *mestres* induce fear and respect through cunning means. Yet the
power of leaders remains pragmatic and active through bodily action,
through aesthetics, through musical prowess, through skill. Despite the
different connotations of power, there is always something more. Capoeira has a hidden spiritual and magic domain that I tried to elucidate
in these pages.

In this epilogue, I would like to briefly talk about knowledge as well.
Knowledge is paramount in capoeira Angola. It is something you learn
in the flesh—with your body, with your personal sacrifice, with your
abilities or inabilities to cope with a treacherous world. Knowledge in
capoeira is presented in multiple ways. A *mestre,* in order to probe himself, needs to master the art of learning constantly about more things
all the time. His knowledge is never systematic, and the way he shares
it with others poses a test for innovation. He must talk about his knowledge while remaining closed, and he must deceive in order to show his
credentials, all the time knowing that he could be betrayed by his close
allies.

The path of a *mestre* resembles the path of the sorcerer (see Stoller
and Olkes 1987). One needs to be careful and cautious about revealing
too much and take precautions against other powerful individuals. A

roda becomes a sacred place for interaction only when it is a place focused on prestige and status. As so many things are at stake, a *mestre* in a *roda* is always exposed to the positive and negative actions of others. Through playfulness, a leader laughs off and hides his innermost feeling of self-preservation. Thus, life as a capoeira *mestre* is never easy. It is full of difficulty, adversity, and good and bad fortune, just like the life of any other human being. What characterizes the *mestre* is his ability to find a cunning solution to problems and to fight against adversities and disappointment with a smile on his face.

For many *mestres,* capoeira is a way of life, a distinctive form of perceiving and living in this world. In this capoeira way of life, *mestres* are always apprentices; they do not stop learning until the end of their lives. That's why they call themselves "ignorant persons." This explicit ignorance is not a false modesty: it forms part of their cultural reality. Due to the deceptive nature of their ritual art form, *mestres* truly doubt their actual knowledge of capoeira. This was a common phrase that Mestre Pastinha said to his students. Although he was considered to be a wise man, he stated in a very Socratic way that, at ninety years of age, he was still learning and trying to understand capoeira. Mestre Pastinha is not the only one I know to have said something similar related to knowledge. Old *mestres* in Salvador make the same kinds of comments.

After dedicating their lives to capoeira, *mestres* are confronted with a paradox. They often discover that the more they learn, the more they become aware they will need more than one life to truly understand the meaning of capoeira Angola. By the time they realize the meaning and secret of capoeira, it is already too late. This is because death is the ultimate act of deception a *mestre* must face. Like many of the capoeira tricks *mestres* perform in their lives, death comes unexpectedly, at a time when they no longer can close their bodies. It is an imminent and fatal attack.

🎵 Glossary

agogô   A double-bell, instrument of the capoeira orchestra
angoleiro   A person who practices capoeira Angola
apertar o jogo   Push the game
arame   A steel wire used as a string for the *berimbau*
armada   A stingray kick without hands. Capoeira move.
arte de lutar sorrindo   The art of fighting with a smile
atabaque   A drum similar to a conga. Part of the capoeira Angola
    music orchestra.
aú   Cartwheel. Capoeira move
axé   Cosmic energy
barracão   Shed
bateria   Capoeira orchestra
batizado   Baptism
benção   Blessing kick. Capoeira move
beriba   Tree from which a *berimbau* is fabricated
berimbau   Musical Bow, key resonant instrument in the capoeira
    orchestra.
cabaça   A hollowed gourd, part of the *berimbau*
cabeçada   Head-butt. Capoeira move.
cair pra dentro do jogador   Go inside, and put pressure on a player
camarás   comrades
Candomblé   Afro-Brazilian religion
capenga   lame or fake capoeira player
capoeirista   capoeira player
caxixi   Rattle made of straw and filled with beans or seeds, part of the
    berimbau
chamada   Call. Capoeira move.
chamada de Cristo de costas   Back Christ *chamada*. Capoeira move
chamada de Cristo de frente   Front Christ *chamada*. Capoeira move
chamada de frente   Front *chamada*. Capoeira move
chapa   Plate kick. Capoeira move
cidade alta   Upper city

cidade baixa   Lower city

cobrar do adversário   Pay back or test an adversary

cognitio sensitiva (latin)   Sensuous knowledge that possesses a quality of truth

contramestra, contramestre   *Mestre*'s second in command

corpo fechado   Closed body

criminais   Criminals

dendé   Cosmic energy that materializes in palm oil

disordeiros   Troublemakers

energia   Energy

feijoada   A Brazilian classic dish made of stewed beans with pork or beef

filho   Son

filhos de santo   Sons of saint. Men initiated into Candomblé.

força   Force

ginga   Basic step in capoeira, consisting of swinging the body from one side to the other

gravata   Neck hold. Capoeira regional move no longer used

gunga   A type of *berimbau*. The lead of the capoeira music orchestra with a hollow deep sound.

jogo   Game

jogo de compadres   Game of comrades

jogos de feijão com arroz   Games of rice and beans

madrinha   Godmother of a capoeira regional player

mãe   Mother

mães de santo   Mothers of saint. Women initiated into Candomblé

malandragem   Roguery

malandro   Rogue

malícia   Cunning, astute, deceptive

maliciosos   Tricky, malicious

mandinga   Indigenous form of power. The spiritual force of a *mestre*.

mandingueiro   Someone who embodies *mandinga*

manha   Trickery

manhoso   Tricky

martelo   Hammer kick. Capoeira move

mato   Forest

medio   A type of berimbau. Part of the capoeira Angola music orchestra

meia lua de costas   Back half-moon kick. Capoeira move

meia lua de frente   Front half-moon kick. Capoeira move

mestre, mestra   Brazilian teacher (masculine and feminine forms)

milonga   Form of dance

moleques   Black youngsters

movimentos de cintura desprezada   Movements of displaced waist. Capoeira regional moves

negativa   Negation. Defensive capoeira move

oficinas   Workshops

ogans   Honorific title in the religion of Candomblé. Men responsible for the ritual music

oricongo   a word synonym of *berimbau* used in the nineteen and early twentieth centuries

orixá   Deity in the Afro-Brazilian religion of Candomblé

pais de santo   Fathers of saint. Male priests of Candomblé

pandeiros   Tambourine

patuá   Amulet. Necklace made of plastic beads

poder   Power

rabo de arraia   Stingray's tail kick. Capoeira move

rasteira   Leg-sweep. Capoeira move

reco-reco   A scraper, instrument of the capoeira Angola orchestra

roda   Ring or circle where a capoeira performance takes place

role   A low turn using the hands. Capoeira move

sapinho   Little toad *chamada*. Capoeira angola move.

terreiros   Ceremonial houses of the Afro-Brazilian religion of Candomblé

tesoura   Scissor kick. Capoeira move

treinel   A title in capoeira Angola's hierarchy. Ranking below contramestre

urucungo   See oricongo. A word synonym of *berimbau* used in the nineteenth and twentieth centuries

vadiação   Vagrancy. Word synonym of capoeira in the first half of the twentieth century

vagabundagem   Vagrancy

valentes   Brave, fearless men

valentões   Tough guys

viola   A type of *berimbau* in the capoeira Angola music orchestra in charge of high pitch improvisation

𝔜 References

Abib, Pedro. 2004. *Capoeira Angola: Cultura Popular e o Jogo Dos Saberes na Roda*. Campinas, São Paulo, Brazil: CMU Publicações.

Abreu, Frederico de. 1999. *Bimba é Bamba, a Capoeira No Ringue*. Salvador, Bahia, Brazil: Instituto Jair Moura.

——. 2002. *O Barracão de Waldemar*. Salvador, Bahia, Brazil: Insituto Jair Moura.

Aceti, Monica. 2013. "Becoming and Remaining a Capoeira Practitioner in Europe: Giving a Meaning to One's Commitment." *Loisir e Societé/Society and Leisure* 36(2): 145–60.

Almeida, Bira. 1986. *Capoeira. A Brazilian Art Form. History, Philosophy and Practice*. Berkeley, CA: North Atlantic Books.

Almeida, Marcelo, Janelle Joseph, Alexandre Palma, and Jorge Soares. 2013. "Marketing Strategies within an African-Brazilian Martial Art." *Sport in Society: Cultures, Commerce, Media, Politics* 16(10): 1346–59.

Anderson, Benedict. 1990. *Language and Power: Exploring Political Cultures in Indonesia*. Ithaca, NY: Cornell University Press.

Appadurai, Arjun. 1986. *The Social Life of Things; Commodities in Cultural Perspective*. Cambridge: Cambridge University Press.

Araújo Caires, Benedito Carlos Libório. 2006. *Capoeira e Mercadoria: Possibilidades Pedagógicas Superadoras*. Salvador, Bahia, Brazil: Monografía em Educação Física, Universidade Federal da Bahia.

Araújo, Rosangela Costa. 1999. "Sou Discípulo Que Aprende, Meu Mestre Me Deu Lição. Tradição e Educação Entre os Angoleiros Bahianos (Anos 80–90)." Master's dissertation, Faculdade de Educação, Universidade de São Paulo, São Paulo, Brazil.

Archetti, Eduardo, and Noel Dyck, eds. 2003. *Sports, Dance and Embodied Identities*. Oxford and New York: Berg.

Arens, William, and Ivan Karp, eds. 1989. *Creativity of Power: Cosmology and Action in African Societies*. Washington, DC: Smithsonian Institution Press.

Assunção, Matthias Röhrig. 2005. *Capoeira: The History of an Afro-Brazilian Martial Art*. London: Routledge.

——. 2014. "Ringue ou Academia? A Emergência Dos Estilos Modernos da Capoeira e seu Contexto Global." *História, Ciências, Saúde-Manguinhos* 21(1): 1–15.

Astuti, Rita, and Maurice Bloch. 2012. "Anthropologists as Cognitive Scientists." *Topics in Cognitive Science* 4(3): 453–61.

Barbosa, Maria José Somerlate. 2005a. "A Mulher na Capoeira." *Arizona Journal of Hispanic Cultural Studies* 9: 9–28.

——. 2005b. "Capoeira: A Gramática do Corpo e a Dança Das Palavras." *Luso-Brazilian Review* 42(1): 78–98.

Bastide, Roger. 1978. *The African Religions of Brazil: Toward a Sociology of the Interpenetration of Civilizations,* translated by Helen Sebba. Baltimore: Johns Hopkins University Press.

Bataille, Georges. 1991. *The Accursed Share: An Essay on General Economy.* Vol. 1 *Consumption.* New York: Zone Books.

Bateson, Gregory. 1987. *Steps to an Ecology of Mind.* New York: Ballantine.

Baudrillard, Jean. 1997. *El Sistema de los Objetos.* Ciudad de Mexico, Mexico: Siglo XXI Editores.

Birth, Kevin. 2008. "The Creation of Coevalness and the Danger of Homochronism." *Journal of the Royal Anthropological Institute* 14: 13–20.

Bloch, Maurice. 1998. *How We Think They Think: Anthropological Approaches to Cognition, Memory, and Literacy.* Boulder, CO: Westview Press.

——. 2011. "The Blob." *Anthropology of This Century* 1: 1–22. http://aotcpress.com/articles/blob/

Bourdieu, Pierre, 1989. "Social 'Space and Symbolic Power.'" *Sociological Theory* 7(1): 14–25.

Brito, Celso de. 2012. "Berimbau's 'Use Value' and 'Exchange Value': Production and Consumption as Symbols of Freedom in Contemporary Global Capoeira Angola." *Vibrant—Virtual Brazilian Anthropology* 9(2): 103–27.

Burlamáqui, Anibal. 1928. *Ginástica Nacional: Capoeiragem Metodizada e Regrada.* Rio de Janeiro, Rio de Janeiro, Brazil: Author's Edition.

Calvino, Italo. 1995. "The Black Sheep." In *Numbers in the Dark and Other Stories,* translated by Tim Parks, 22–24. London: Vintage Classics, eBooks.

Capoeira, Nestor. 2003. *The Little Capoeira Book,* rev. ed. Berkeley, CA: North Atlantic Books.

Carneiro, Edison. 1977. *Capoeira, Cadernos do Folklore No. 1.* Rio de Janeiro, Rio de Janeiro, Brazil: FUNARTE.

Cascudo, Luís Câmara. 1967. *Folclore do Brasil.* Rio de Janeiro Rio de Janeiro, Brazil: Fondo de Cultura.

Coutinho, Daniel. 1993. *O ABC da Capoeira Angola, Os Manuscritos de Mestre Noronha.* Brasília, Distrito Federal, Brazil: Governo do Distrito Federal.

Cruz, Jose Luis Oliveira (Mestre Bola Sete). 2006. *Historias e Estorias da Capoeiragem.* Salvador, Bahia, Brazil: P555 Editores.

Csordas, Thomas. 1990. "Embodiment as a Paradigm for Anthropology." *Ethos* 18(1): 5–47.

DaMatta, Roberto. 1991. *Carnivals, Rogues, and Heroes: An Interpretation of the Brazilian Dilemma,* translated by John Drury. Notre Dame, IN: University of Notre Dame Press.

Decanio, Filho Angelo A. (Mestre Decanio). 1997. *A Herança de Pastinha*. Coleção São Salomão, 3, Salvador, Bahia, Brasil: Author's edition.

———. 2001a. "As Raízes da Regional." *Revista da Bahia* 33 (*Capoeira, Ginástica da Resistência*): 33–41.

———. 2001b. "Pastinha, o Mestre dos Mestres." *Revista da Bahia número* 33 (*Capoeira, Ginástica da Resistência*): 86–99.

———. 2001c. "Transe capoeirano: estado de consciência modificado na capoeira." *Revista da Bahia número* 33 (*Capoeira, Ginástica da Resistência*): 42–65.

Delamont, Sara. 2006. "The Smell of Sweat and Rum: Authority and Authenticity in Capoeira Classes." *Ethnography and Education* 1(2): 161–76.

Delamont, Sara, and Neil Stephens. 2007. "Excruciating Elegance: Representing the Embodied Habitus of Capoeira." Working paper. Cardiff University Press, ESRC National Center for Research Methods, and Economic and Social Research Council, Cardiff, Wales.

———. 2008. "Up on the Roof: The Embodied Habitus of Diasporic Capoeira." *Cultural Sociology* 2(1): 57–74.

Deleuze, Gilles, and Félix Guattari. 1987. *A Thousand Plateaus: Capitalism and Schizophrenia*, translated by Brian Massumi. Minneapolis: University of Minnesota Press.

Desch-Obi, Thomas J. 2000. "Engolo: Combat Traditions in African and African Diasporas History." Doctoral thesis, University of California Los Angeles.

Descola, Philippe. 1988. *La Selva Culta: Simbolismo y Praxis en la Ecología de los Achuar*, translated by Juan Carrera Collin and Xavier Catta Quelen. Peru: IFEA y ABYA-YALA.

———. 2005. *Par-delà Nature et Culture*. Paris: Gallimard.

Dias, Adriana Albert. 2004. "A Malandragem da Mandinga, o Cotidiano dos Capoeiras em Salvador na Republica Velha (1910–1925)." Master's dissertation, Universidade Federal da Bahia, Salvador, Bahia, Brazil.

———. 2006. *Mandinga, Manha e Malícia: Uma História Sobre os Capoeiras na Capital da Bahia (1910–1925)*. Salvador, Bahia, Brazil: Editorial da Universidade Federal da Bahia.

Dossar, Kenneth 1992. "Capoeira Angola: Dancing between Two Worlds." *Afro-Hispanic Review* 11(1–3): 5–11.

Downey, Greg. 2002. "Listening to Capoeira: Phenomenology, Embodiment, and the Materiality of Music." *Ethnomusicology* 46(3): 487–509.

———. 2005. *Learning Capoeira: Lessons in Cunning from an Afro-Brazilian Art*. Oxford: Oxford University Press.

———. 2008. "Scaffolding Imitation in Capoeira: Physical Education and Enculturation in an Afro-Brazilian Art." *American Anthropologist* 110(2): 204–13.

———. 2010. "Domesticating an Urban Menace: Reforming Capoeira as a Brazilian National Sport." *International Journal of the History of Sport* 19(4): 1–32.

Durkheim, Emile. 1995. *The Elementary Forms of Religious Life,* translated by Karen E. Fields. New York: The Free Press.

Duvignaud, Jean. 1979. *El Sacrificio Inútil.* Mexico City, Mexico: Fondo de Cultura Económica.

———. 1982. *El Juego del Juego.* Mexico City, Mexico: Fondo de Cultura Económica.

Fabian, Johannes. 1983. *Time and the Other: How Anthropology Makes Its Object.* New York: Columbia University Press.

Falcão, José Luiz Cirqueira. 2005. "Fluxos e Refluxos da Capoeira: Brasil e Portugal Gingando na Roda." *Analise Social* 40(174): 111–33.

Faria, Lázaro [Director]. 2005. *Mandinga em Manhattan.* DVD. Salvador, Bahia, Brazil: Casa de Cinema Da Bahia.

Farias, Rodrigo da Costa e Goellner, and Silvana Vilodre. 2007. "A Capoeira do Mercado Modelo de Salvador: Gestualidades Performáticas de Corpos em Exibição." *Revista Brasileira de Educação Física e Esporte* 21(2): 143–55.

Fonseca, Vivian Luiz. 2008. "A Capoeira Contemporânea: Antigas Questões, Novos Desafíos." *Recorde: Revista de História do Esporte* 1(1): 1–30.

Foucault, Michel. 1980. *Microfísica del Poder.* Madrid, Spain: Ediciones de la Piqueta.

———. 1988. "El Sujeto y el Poder." *Revista Mexicana de Sociología* 50(3): 3–20.

———. 1999. *Estrategias de Poder: Obras Esenciales, Volumen II.* Barcelona, Spain: Paidós Editores.

Freeman, Luke. 2007. "Why Are Some People Powerful?" In *Questions of Anthropology,* edited by Rita Astuti, Jonathan Parry, and Charles Stafford, 281–306. London: Berg.

Fryer, Peter. 2000. *Rhythms of Resistance: African Musical Heritage in Brazil.* London: Pluto Press.

Gadamer, Hans-Georg. 1986. *The Relevance of the Beautiful and Other Essays,* translated by Nicholas Walker, edited by Robert Bernasconi. Cambridge: Cambridge University Press.

Geertz, Clifford. 1993. *Local Knowledge.* London: Fontana Press.

———. 2000. *The Interpretation of Cultures. Selected Essays.* New York City, New York: Basic Books.

Gell, Alfred. 1998. *Art and Agency. An Anthropological Theory.* Oxford, UK: Clarendon Press.

Godelier, Maurice. 1986. *The Making of Great Men: Male Domination and Power among the New Guinea Baruya.* Cambridge, UK: Cambridge University Press.

Goldman, Marcio. 2005. "Formas do Saber e Modos do Ser: Observações Sobre Multiplicidade e Ontologia no Candomblé." *Religião e Sociedade* 25(2): 102–21.

———. 2008. "How to Learn in an Afro-Brazilian Spirit Possession Religion: Ontology and Multiplicity in Candomblé." In *Learning Religion: Anthropological Approaches,* edited by David Berliner and Ramon Sarró, 103–19. New York: Berghahn Books.

González Varela, Sergio. 2012a. "Cosmología, Simbolismo y Práctica; El Concepto de 'Cuerpo Cerrado' en el Ritual de la Capoeira Angola." *Revista Maguaré, dossier de Ritos y Juegos* 26(2): 119–46.

———. 2012b. "La Expansión Global de la Capoeira: Trazando Conexiones en Movimiento." In *Sujetos Emergentes: Nuevos y Viejos Contextos de Negociación de las Identidades en América Latina,* edited by Carlos Alberto Casas Mendoza and José Guadalupe Rivera González y Leonardo Ernesto Márquez Mireles, 111–30. Mexico City, Mexico: Ediciones Eón y UASLP.

———. 2012c. "Una Mirada Antropológica a la Estética y Personificación de los Objetos. El Caso de la Capoeira Angola en Brasil." *Revista Desacatos* 40: 127–40.

———. 2013. "*Mandinga*: Power and Deception in Afro-Brazilian Capoeira." *Social Analysis: International Journal of Social and Cultural Practice* 57(2): 1–20.

Graham, Richard. 1991. "Technology and Culture Change: The Development of the 'Berimbau' in Colonial Brazil." *Latin American Music Review/Revista de Música Latinoamericana* 12(1): 1–20.

Greimas, Algirdas. 1997. *De la imperfección.* Mexico City, Mexico: Fondo de Cultura Económica.

Griffith, Lauren Miller. 2016. *In Search of Legitimacy: How Outsiders Become Part of the Afro-Brazilian Capoeira Tradition.* New York and Oxford: Berghahn Books.

Grupo de Capoeira Angola Pelourinho (GCAP). 2003. *Capoeira Angola 2,* Leafleat CD Vol. 2. Salvador, Bahia, Brazil.

Grupo de Capoeira Angola Pelourinho (GCAP), and Associação de Capoeira Navio Negreiro (ACANNE). 1989. "Capoeira Angola/Resistência Negra." *Revista Exu, Fundação Casa Jorge Amado, No. 11,* 33–43. Salvador, Bahia, Brazil.

Guizardi, Menara. 2011. "Genuinamente brasileña: La Nacionalización y Expansión de la Capoeira como Práctica Social en Brasil." *Revista Araucaria* 26: 72–100.

Handelman, Don. 1990. *Models and Mirrors: Towards an Anthropology of Public Events.* Cambridge, UK: Cambridge University Press.

———. 2008. "Afterword: Returning to Cosmology—Thoughts on the Positioning of Belief." *Social Analysis* 52(1): 181–95.

Handelman, Don, and Galina Lindquist. 2005. *Ritual in Its Own Right: Exploring the Dynamics of Transformation.* New York and Oxford: Berghahn Books.

Harris, Marvin. 1974. *Cows, Pigs, Wars, and Witches: The Riddles of Culture.* New York: Random House.

———. 1978. *Cannibals and Kings: The Origins of Cultures.* London: Collins.

Hedegard, Danielle. 2012. "Becoming a Capoeirista: A Situational Approach to Interpreting a Foreign Cultural Good." *Sociological Inquiry* 20 (10): 1–22.

———. 2013. "Blackness and Experience in Omnivorous Cultural Consumption: Evidence from the Tourism of Capoeira in Salvador, Brazil." *Poetics: Journal of Empirical Research on Culture, the Media and the Arts* 41(1): 1–26.

Henare A., M. Holbraad and S. Wastell, eds. 2007. *Thinking through Things: Theorising Artefacts Ethnographically.* London: Routledge.

Holbraad, Martin. 2008a. "Definitive Evidence, from Cuban Gods." *Journal of the Royal Anthropological Institute* (Special Issue *Objects of Evidence*), ed. Matthew Engelke: Vol. 14, Issue Supplement S1: S93–S109.

———. 2008b. "Against the Motion." In *'Ontology' Is Just Another Word for 'Culture.' Group for Debates in Anthropological Theory,* edited by Soumhya Venkatesan, 32–39. Manchester, UK: University of Manchester Press.

———. 2011. "Can the Thing Speak?" *OAP Press, Working Paper Series* 7: 1–26.

———. 2012. *Truth in Motion: The Recursive Anthropology of Cuban Divination.* Chicago: University of Chicago Press.

Ingold, Tim, ed. 2005. *Key Debates in Anthropology.* London: Routledge.

Itapoan, César (director unknown). 1988. *Entrevista com Mestre Waldemar,* DVD, Instituto Jair Moura, Salvador, Bahia, Brazil.

———. (director unknown) 1990. *Entrevista com Mestre Caiçara.* DVD, Instituto Jair Moura, Salvador, Bahia, Brazil.

Jackson, Michael. 1983. "Knowledge of the Body." *Man* 18(2), 327–45.

Joas, Hans. 1996. *The Creativity of Action.* Cambridge, UK: Polity Press.

Jornal Diário de Notícias. 1911, 24 October. Bahia, Brazil.

Joseph, Janelle. 2005. "Trangressing Boundaries and Crossing Borders: As Capoeiristas Brasileiras (Female Brazilian Practitioners of an Afro-Brazilian Martial Art)." *Women and Environments International Magazine* 68/69: 31–33.

———. 2008. "'Going to Brazil': Transational and Corporeal Movements of a Canadian-Brazilian Martial Arts Community." *Global Networks: A Journal of Transnational Affairs* 8(2): 194–213.

———. 2012. "The Practice of Capoeira: Diasporic Black Culture in Canada." *Ethnic and Racial Studies* 35(6): 1078–95.

Kapferer, Bruce. 2007. "Sorcery and the Beautiful: A Discourse on the Aesthetics of Ritual." In *Aesthetics in Performance: Formation of Symbolic Construction and Experience,* edited by Angela Hobart and Bruce Kapferer, 129–60. New York and Oxford: Berghahn Books.

Karp, Ivan, and Dismas Masolo, eds. 2000. *African Philosophy as Cultural Inquiry.* Bloomington: Indiana University Press.

Kohn, Tamara. 2003. "The Aikido Body: Expressions of Group Identities and Self-Discovery in Martial Arts Training." In *Sports, Dance and Embodied Identities,* edited by Eduardo Archetti and Dyck Noel, 139–57. Oxford and New York: Berg.

Latour, Bruno. 1993. *We Have Never Been Modern.* Cambridge, MA: Harvard University Press.

———. 2002. *Reflexão Sobre o Culto Moderno dos Deuses Fe(i)tiches.* Bauru, São Paulo, Brazil: EDUSC.

———. 2005. *Reassembling the Social: An Introduction to Actor–Network Theory.* Oxford, UK: Oxford University Press.

Lévy-Bruhl, Levy. 1923. *Primitive Mentality.* New York: Macmillan.

Lewis, Lowell. 1992. *Ring of Liberation: Deceptive Discourse in Brazilian Capoeira.* Chicago and London: University of Chicago Press.

———. 1995. "Genre and Embodiment: From Brazilian Capoeira to the Ethnology of Human Movement." *Cultural Anthropology* 10(2): 221–43.

———. 1999. "Sex and Violence in Brazil: 'Carnaval, Capoeira,' and the Problem of Everyday Life." *American Ethnologist* 26(3): 539–57.

Luhmann, Niklas. 2005. *Poder.* Mexico City, Mexico: Universidad Iberoamericana y Anthropos.

MacLennan, Janet. 2011. "'To Build a Beautiful Dialogue': Capoeira as Contradiction." *Journal of International and Intercultural Communication* 4(2): 146–62.

Magalhães, Paulo Andrade 2011. "Jogo de Discursos: A Disputa por a Hegemonia na Tradição da Capoeira Angola Baiana." Master's dissertation. Salvador, Bahia, Brazil: Universidade Federal da Bahia.

Matory, James Lorand. 2005. *Black Atlantic Religion: Tradition, Transnationalism, and Matriarchy in the Afro-Brazilian Candomblé.* Princeton, NJ: Princeton University Press.

Mauss, Marcel. 2002. *The Gift: The Form and Reason for Exchange in Archaic Societies.* London: Routledge.

———. 2005. *A General Theory of Magic,* translated by Robert Brain. London: Routledge.

Merleau-Ponty, Maurice. 2005. *Phenomenology of Perception,* translated by Colin Smith. London: Routledge.

Merrel, Floyd. 2005. *Capoeira and Candomblé: Conformity and Resistance through Afro-Brazilian Experience.* Princeton, NJ: Markus Wiener.

Moraes, Pedro. 2000. "Entrevista com Mestre Moraes." *Revista Praticando Capoeira* 1(2): 12–15.

Morefield, John. 2008. "Capoeira Angola and the Novels of Jorge Amado." *Aethlon: Journal of Sports Literature* 25(2): 1–16.

Mosko, Mark. 2010. "Deep Holes: Fractal Holography in Trobriand Agency and Culture." In *Experiments in Holism: Theory and Practice in Contemporary Anthropology,* edited by Ton Otto and Nils Bubandt, 150–74. London: Wiley-Blackwell.

Moura, Jair. 1991. *Mestre Bimba, a Crônica da Capoeiragem.* Salvador, Bahia, Brazil: Fundação Mestre Bimba.

———. 2005. *Os Pioneiros do Renascimento da Capoeiragem Angola.* Salvador, Bahia, Brazil: Inédito.

Muricy, Carlos Antonio [director]. 1998. *Pastinha, uma vida pela capoeira.* DVD, Salvador, Bahia, Brazil.

Nietzsche, Friedrich. 2011. *La Voluntad de Poder: Ensayo Sobre una Transmutación de Todos los Valores.* Mexico City, Mexico: Grupo Editorial Tomo. Originally published in 1901.

Oliveira, Josivaldo Pires de. 2005. *No Tempo dos Valentes: Os Capoeiras na Cidade da Bahia*. Salvador, Bahia, Brazil: Quarteto Editora.

Oliveira, Josivaldo Pires de, and Pinheiro Luiz Augusto Leal. 2009. *Capoeira, Identidade e Género: Ensaios Sobre a História Social da Capoeira no Brasil*. Salvador, Bahia, Brazil: Editora da Universidade Federal da Bahia.

Paiva, Ilnete Porpino. 2007. "A Capoeira e os Mestres." Doctoral dissertation in social sciences. Universidade Federal do Rio Grande do Norte, Natal, Brazil.

Palmié, Stephan, and Charles Stewart. 2016. "Introduction: For an Anthropology of History." *HAU: Journal of Ethnographic Theory* 6(1): 207–36.

Parés, Luis Nicolau. 2006. *A Formação do Candomblé: História e Ritual da Nação Jeje na Bahia*. Campinas, São Paulo, Brazil: Editora da UNICAMP.

Pastinha, Vicente Ferreira. 1996. *Manuscritos e Desenho de Mestre Pastinha*, organized by Ângelo Decanio. Salvador, Bahia, Brazil: Own Edition.

Pires, A. L. Cardoso. 2002. *Bimba, Pastinha e Besouro de Mangangá, Três Personagens da Capoeira Baiana*. Araguaína, Tocantins, Brazil: Fundação Universidade do Tocantins.

Rapport, Nigel. 2003. *I Am Dynamite: An Alternative Anthropology of Power*. London: Routledge.

Rector, Mónica. 2008. "Capoeira: El Lenguaje Silencioso de los Gestos." *Signo y Pensamiento* 52(27): 184–94.

Rego, Waldeloir. 1968. *Capoeira Angola. Ensaio Sócio-etnográfico*. Salvador, Bahia, Brazil: Editóra Itapuá, Coleção Baiana.

Reis, Letícia Vidor de Sousa. 2000. *O Mundo de Pernas para o ar: A Capoeira no Brasil*. São Paulo, São Paulo, Brazil: Publisher Brasil.

Risério, Antonio. 2004. *Uma Historia da Cidade da Bahia*. Rio de Janeiro, Rio de Janeiro, Brazil: Versal Editores.

Robitaille, Laurence. 2014. "Promoting *Capoeira*, Branding Brazilian: A Focus on the Semantic Body." *Black Music Research Journal* 34(2): 229–54.

Rosario, Claudio de Campos, Neil Stephens, and Sara Delamont. 2010. "'I Am Your Teacher, I Am Brazilian!' Authenticity and Authority in European Capoeira." *Sports, Education and Society* 15(1): 103–20.

Sahlins, Marshall. 1963. "Poor Man, Rich Man, Big Man, Chief: Political Types in Melanesia and Polynesia." *Comparative Studies in Society and History* 5(3): 285–303.

———. 1976. *Culture and Practical Reason*. Chicago and London: University of Chicago Press.

Santos, Marcelino dos (Mestre Mau). 1990. *Capoeira e Mandingas: Cobrinha Verde*. Salvador, Bahia, Brazil: Apoio Cultural Filhos de Bimba e Liceu de Artes e Ofícios da Bahia.

Shaffer, Kay. 1977. *O Berimbau-de-barriga e Seus Toques*. Funarte, Rio de Janeiro, Rio de Janeiro, Brazil: Instituto Nacional do Folclore.

Silva, Alberto da Costa. 1994. "O Brasil, a África eo Atlântico no Século XIX." *Estudos Avançados* 8(21): 21–42.

Silva, Washington Bruno da (Mestre Canjiquinha). 1989. *Canjiquinha, Alegria da Capoeira*. Salvador, Bahia, Brazil: A Rasteira Editora.

Soares, Eugênio. 2001. *A Capoeira Escrava e Outras Tradições Rebeldes no Rio de Janeiro: 1808–1850*. Campinas, São Paulo, Brazil: Editora da UNICAMP.

Sperber, Dan. 1996. *Explaining Culture: A Naturalistic Approach*. Oxford, UK: Blackwell.

———. 2000. *Metarepresentations: A Multidisciplinary Perspective*. Oxford, UK: Oxford University Press.

Stephens, Neil, and Sara Delamont. 2009. "They Start to Get Malicia." *British Journal of Sociology of Education* 30(5): 537–48.

Stoller, Paul. 1989. *Fusion of the Worlds*. Chicago: University of Chicago Press.

Stoller, Paul, and Cheryl Olkes. 1987. *In Sorcery's Shadow: A Memoir of Apprenticeship among the Songhay of Niger*. Chicago: University of Chicago Press.

Strathern, Andrew. 2007. *The Rope of Moka: Big Men and Ceremonial Exchange in Mount Hagen, New Guinea*. Cambridge, UK: Cambridge University Press.

Strathern, Marilyn. 1990. *The Gender of the Gift: Problems with Women and Problems with Society in Melanesia*. Berkeley: University of California Press.

———. 1995. "The Nice Thing about Culture Is That Everyone Has It." In *Shifting Contexts: Transformations in Anthropological Knowledge*, edited by Marilyn Strathern, 153–76. London: Routledge.

———. 1999. *Property, Substance, and Effect: Anthropological Essays on Persons and Things*. London: Athlone Press.

———. 2004. *Partial Connections*. Updated ed. Oxford, UK: Altamira Press. Originally published.

Talmon-Chvaicer, Maya. 2008. *The Hidden History of Capoeira: A Collision of Cultures in the Brazilian Battle Dance*. Austin: University of Texas Press.

Thompson, Robert Farris. 1991. *Dancing between Two Worlds: Kongo-Angola; Culture and the Americas*. New York: African Diaspora Institute.

Turner, Victor. 1982. *From Ritual to Theatre, the Human Seriousness of Play*. New York: Paj Publications.

———. 1986. "Body, Brain and Culture", *Performing Arts Journal*, 10 (2): 26–34.

Vassallo, Ponde Simone. 2005. "As Novas Versões da África no Brasil: A Busca das 'Tradições Africanas' e as Relações entre Capoeira e Candomblé." *Religião e Sociedade* 25 (2): 161–89.

Vieira, Luis Renato. 1996. *O Jogo da Capoeira: Corpo e Cultura Popular no Brasil*. Rio de Janeiro, Rio de Janeiro, Brazil: Sprint Editora.

Viveiros de Castro, Eduardo. 1998. "Cosmological Deixis and Amerindian Perspectivism." *Journal of the Royal Anthropological Institute* 4(3): 469–88.

———. 2004. "Perspectival Anthropology and the Method of Controlled Equivocations." *Tipití: Journal of the Society for the Anthropology of Lowland South America* 2(1): 3–22.

———. 2010. *Metafísicas Caníbales: Líneas de Antropología Postestructural*. Buenos Aires, Buenos Aires, Argentina: Katz Editores.

Wacquant, Loic. 2006. *Body and Souls, Notebooks on an Apprenticeship Boxer.* Oxford, UK: Oxford University Press.

Wafer, Jim W. 1991. *The Taste of Blood: Spirit Possession in Brazilian Candomblé.* Philadelphia: University of Pennsylvania Press.

Wagner, Roy. 1972. *Habu: The Innovation of Meaning in Daribi Religion.* Chicago: University of Chicago Press.

———. 1981. *The Invention of Culture.* Rev. and expanded ed. Chicago: University of Chicago Press.

———. 1986a. *Symbols That Stand for Themselves.* Chicago: University of Chicago Press.

———. 1986b. *Asiwinarong: Ethos, Imagen and Social Power among the Usen Baron of New Ireland.* Princeton, NJ: Princeton University Press.

———. 1991. "The Fractal Person." In *Big Men and Great Men: Personications of Power in Melanesia,* edited by Maurice Godelier and Marilyn Strathern, 159–73. Cambridge, UK: Cambridge University Press.

———. 2001. *An Anthropology of the Subject: Holographic Worldview in New Guinea and its Meaning and Significance for the World of Anthropology.* Berkeley: University of California Press.

Weber, Max. 1947. *The Theory of Social and Economical Organization,* translated by Arthur M. Henderson and Talcott Parsons. Glencoe, IL: Free Press and Falcon's Wing Press.

———. 1978. *Economy and Society: An Outline of Interpretive Sociology.* Reprint edited by Guenther Roth and Claus Wittich. Berkeley, Los Angeles, and London: University of California Press. Originally published 1922.

Weiner, James F. 1988. *The Heart of the Pearl Shell: The Mythological Dimension of Foi Sociality.* Berkeley: University of California Press.

Zonzon, Christine Nicole. 2007. "A Roda de Capoeira Angola: Os Sentidos em Jogo." Master's dissertation, Universidade Federal da Bahia, Salvador, Bahia, Brazil.

———. 2014. *Nas Pequenas e Grandes Rodas de Capoeira e da Vida.* PhD Dissertation, Faculdade de Filosofia e Ciências Humanas, Universidade Federal da Bahia, Salvador, Bahia, Brazil.

Index